Bitter Sweet

Bitter Sweet

Stefan Popper

The Book Guild Ltd

First published in Great Britain in 2018 by
The Book Guild Ltd
9 Priory Business Park
Wistow Road, Kibworth
Leicestershire, LE8 0RX
Freephone: 0800 999 2982
www.bookguild.co.uk
Email: info@bookguild.co.uk
Twitter: @bookguild

Typeset in Aldine401 BT

Printed and bound in Great Britain by CPI Group (UK) Ltd, Croydon, CR0 4YY

ISBN 978 1912362 356

British Library Cataloguing in Publication Data.
A catalogue record for this book is available from the British Library.

Published in memory of Stefan and Lisa and dedicated to refugees everywhere.

Stefan Popper died on 16 March 2016. He is survived by his wife, Wendy and three remaining children Sue, Ross & Geoff, who together wrote this dedication.

Contents

Foreword

I would like to thank all the people who have encouraged me to persevere with my writing, and who have taken the time and trouble to read this book and make comments. I am reluctant to mention names as there is the danger that I will leave someone out, and so I will not do so – with just one exception. I cannot thank my wife Wendy enough for her help. She has spent hours reading drafts and making suggestions to improve wording and presentation to make the book more readable. In the end, however, I take responsibility for the book, good or bad.

Any existing copyright in photographs and drawings is acknowledged. If someone can provide evidence of ownership and wishes to be acknowledged by name I will do so in any future editions.

1

Vienna: Family Background

Twins were not on the mind of my mother or her doctor when, in Vienna, Austria, she was in labour on 8th May 1932. To everyone's surprise, just eleven minutes after I was born, my sister Lisa arrived. We were her only children.

Margarethe Popper (Mutti) with the twins: Stefan and Lisa

I can prove I was born in two different places! My original birth certificate states that I was born in Vienna IX Loblichgasse 14, but when I obtained certified copies I found to my surprise that these said I was born at my home address. The IKG[1] had decided that it made more sense to use the permanent home address rather than the transient birth address on the certificates. I can see an argument for this, but do not like the breach of principle.

My paternal and maternal grandparents were Jewish and can be traced to the Czech Republic, Slovakia and Hungary, but moved to Vienna before my parents were born. My paternal grandfather had been a wine merchant in a company called Stern and Popper. In December 1914 my maternal grandfather and his brother-in-law had co-founded the Café Herrenhof in the centre of Vienna, and had prospered.

My father had been immensely proud of Vienna and Austria. His parents named him Franz Ferdinand – a name he shared with the Crown Prince of the Austrian-Hungarian Empire whose assassination in 1914 sparked the First World War. My father volunteered and fought on the Russian Front, was commissioned as a second lieutenant in the reserve and remained so until he was summarily dismissed by the Nazis. After the war he qualified as a lawyer, practising in Vienna.

My mother was well educated but as far as I know had no professional qualifications. She worked informally at the Café Herrenhof at times. She had a younger brother Johannes, known as Hans. Like me, my dad had a younger sister, Martha, and there will be more about them both later.

I understand that there was a good bit of anti-Semitism in Austria but nevertheless the professions and military were open to Jews, at least in my father's experience. There were predominantly Jewish areas in Vienna, but there appeared to be no restrictions as to where one could live as we lived in the First or Inner District of Vienna.

My parents enjoyed the social life of the city. My mother, whom we called Mutti, loved dancing and they both enjoyed going to the opera and had access to season tickets so they could go whenever they wanted.

There was a strong café culture in Vienna and I think a lot of entertainment may have taken place away from home. In the café people socialised, read the papers, played bridge and chess, listened to music and

---

1   Israelitische Kultusgemeinde.

danced, and no doubt set the world to rights while enjoying the delicious cakes or sampling one of the numerous varieties of coffee which were on offer. It was an elegant, well-ordered and cultured existence, though there were also major political tensions.

Maximilian Popper, my paternal grandfather, died in 1936 of natural causes. His widow Anna (née Benda) committed suicide on 18th March 1938. As her death occurred within six days of the Nazi annexation she has been classed as a Holocaust victim. She is buried with her husband in the Jewish part of the Central Cemetery (the main cemetery in Vienna)[2].

---

2   Group 22, Row 18, Number 25. Access is via Gate 4 of the cemetery, which is vast.

2

1932–1938: Early Childhood Memories

My parents married in June 1927 and moved into a large flat on the fourth floor of a block of flats known as Mozart House at Number 8 Rauhensteingasse, Vienna 1. This narrow street is parallel to the Kaerntnerstrasse, one of the inner city's main thoroughfares.

The house was located on the site where Mozart lived when he wrote *The Magic Flute*, and where he died. The association with Mozart had a major disadvantage as a bust of him was located in the stairwell, preventing the installation of a lift. As my father had his practice in the flat I wonder what some of his clients must have thought of the climb.

The facade of the building still exists but the interior has vanished into a department store. The bust is now displayed within the store. There is a café at the top of the building where my daughter Sue and I sat in 2002, imagining we were in the area where our flat had once been.

The 140-square-metre flat was expensively furnished. Mutti's bedroom was in Irish birch. Solid mahogany was used for the dining-room furniture, which must have been large as the dining table could be extended to seat eighteen people. One of the rooms was in the Adam style, modelled on a room in a Kensington museum. Another was in the Chippendale style, with walnut furniture. Yet another room was furnished in leather. Expensive Persian carpets had been given as wedding presents. My mother must have loved it!

The children's room was on two levels, so that we slept on one level and were able to play on the other. I remember sleeping in cots with the sides up. They must have been quite big as we were six when we left Vienna.

In this room too, I built what seemed to me a most beautiful city made from wooden bricks. We placed real candles on it, and when they were lit it was a wondrous sight to my eyes. I still love seeing cities lit up at night.

It was traditional around Christmas for children to be given a figure called a 'Grampus', which was made of dried fruit and nuts and was made to look like a devil. Whilst Lisa kept her Grampus in pristine condition, I took bites out of the fruit, and in order to restore them to their original size, hit them hard to flatten and enlarge them.

One Christmas we waited excitedly outside one of the reception rooms to see the Christmas tree which had been placed there. When we were allowed in I saw this wonderful tree from floor to ceiling, decorated and illuminated with real candles. There probably were presents beneath it, but it is the tree I remember.

Mutti told me that the family used to have a meat-free day each week. We must have enjoyed schnitzels too, but the regular evening meal of semolina pudding with a square of chocolate in the centre is my only memory of food. How I enjoyed starting from the cooler outside as we had been taught and working my way in to the chocolate!

We had our share of illnesses, including middle-ear infections, and tummy aches soothed with hot-water bottles or an adult lying next to us with a hand on our tummy to warm it. It seemed to work.

Bed rest was the treatment of choice if one had a temperature, which was measured unpleasantly but accurately with a rectal thermometer. Tummy troubles were also treated with enemas – real ones with long rubber tubes and warm soapy water. I cannot remember who inflicted these upon us, but they were not popular.

Polio was a feared illness, and one morning I could not be roused. Mutti feared the worst, but just as the doctor arrived I woke up none the worse for a good night's sleep.

On another occasion I bit off a piece out of the glass I was drinking from. There was great concern and I was made to eat loads of sauerkraut in the vain hope that it would enmesh the piece of glass. As is common with such incidents, nothing untoward happened.

I can remember one nursery song which started with the words *Wenn*

Ich gross bin Liebe Mutter. The child says that when he is grown he will care for his mother and do everything for her. Strange as it may seem, in some ways that vow almost came true for me.

Mutti used to say that if we did not behave she would tell our dad and he would express a *Macht Wort*, which means a 'word of power'. This was usually enough to bring us back into line. I cannot remember my dad smacking me, but I was scared of what would happen if he was told of any misbehaviour. One can deduce, therefore, that I was naughty at times, but I also remember that I was described as having a *Butter Herz* (heart of butter)!

I cannot remember any particular friends, but must have had some as on one occasion I introduced a little girl to someone as my future wife!

We were taken for walks in the parks of Vienna. I expect it was usually our nanny who took us, but I have a photograph of us with Opapa[3] in the Volksgarten.

Lisa and I were often dressed in identical clothes including sailor outfits, and we also had lovely dark blue overcoats to wear. I apparently liked puddles and enjoyed walking through them or even throwing myself into them, which I assume was classed as naughty.

Once when we were out I had to go to the toilet urgently, and ended up going outdoors as there was no toilet nearby. A park keeper who happened to see us was very angry and made the nanny clean up after me. I am sure this was an accident and not deliberate naughtiness.

On another occasion, which must have been after the Nazi annexation, I was riding my scooter. There was an SA[4] man, a brown-shirted Nazi, sitting on a bench, and I scooted enthusiastically back and forth giving a Nazi salute. I was moved on quickly by our nanny as it must have been thought dangerous for me to engage in this sort of activity.

Before we left Vienna we were starting to learn to skate. I enjoyed going to the rink at the Stadtpark, but it could get crowded. We were just beginning to learn simple figure-of-eight skating. I strongly suspect that this rink became closed to us following the Nazi annexation because we were taken to a smaller rink, probably early in the day as I remember it being in pristine condition and so more difficult to skate on.

---

3   Opapa is the German equivalent of 'grandad' and is the term I use for my maternal grandfather. Omama is the term I use for my maternal grandmother.

4   Sturmabteilung (Storm Section), – the original paramilitary wing of the Nazi Party (otherwise known as 'Brownshirts').

Lisa and Stefan, July 1934

I am sure we must have been taken to the Prater, a large, permanent amusement park in Vienna with many attractions for children and adults including a very large Ferris wheel. When Lisa and I were in Vienna in June 1997 we spent some time there and sat in an open-air café listening to Austrian music.

Prior to the Nazi annexation we would have been taken to the Café Herrenhof, and I vaguely remember being near a serving counter and being given whipped cream to eat. Opapa, who was diabetic and on a very strict diet, used to have special, very light diabetic rolls. I longed in vain to taste these, but later in life when I at last got the chance I found they were pretty awful.

Manners were important and children were expected to 'kiss the hand' when meeting adults. It was rude to use adult forms of greeting, and when I tried it once I got told off. It would also have been unheard of for a child to address an adult by their given name without a prefix such as Aunt or Uncle.

Vienna was and is a beautiful city with lots of churches. One even bore my name, being St. Stephan's Cathedral.[5] Lisa was less fortunate, but we must have seen the Votive Church, a neo-Gothic structure with two identical spires, which we named the Stefan and Lisa Spires. This was obviously fairer from the perspective of twins.

In the heat of the summer we were taken away on holiday. We really liked a place where there was a ruined castle; I think it was called Rauhenstein. I was not so keen on Voeslau, a summer resort near Vienna. Perhaps it did not have such an interesting castle to climb about on.

All in all, I think we had a happy childhood in Vienna.

---

5   I have always thought it was spelt Stefan, but it seems that Stephan is more likely.

Stefan and Lisa, May 1936

Stefan and Lisa 1937

3

The Arrival of the Nazis

On 12ᵗʰ March 1938 the Nazis annexed Austria and everything changed. I can remember seeing what probably was their parade into Vienna, which to my child's eyes looked fantastic.

Lisa recalls that sometime after the annexation we were hidden for a short while by Mutti's friend Alice Fischer, who lived in a villa on the outskirts of Vienna.

I was always very keen to listen to adult conversation, but my parents did not want me to overhear things which they thought were unsuitable or perhaps unsafe for me to hear. I can recall them addressing each other in Czechoslovakian[6] with a sentence which meant something like 'not in front of the children'. I expect at times we could sense increased secrecy and tension.

I think my father had realised very early on that the only safe thing was to try and get out of Austria. On 15ᵗʰ March 1938, just three days after the annexation, his parents-in-law were forbidden to enter their own Café Herrenhof following a very traumatic meeting at which both my parents had also been present. That day a search was also undertaken by the Nazis at our home. I remember Mutti telling me years later that she and Dad had spent time destroying foreign currency notes which presumably they were not allowed to hold, so perhaps they were anticipating a search.

It was evening. I was in bed and recall footsteps outside the bedroom.

---

6   It is not clear whether this was Czech or Slovak.

I seem to remember jumping up and down in bed with excitement and curiosity. Perhaps there were also voices which alerted me. I imagine having an excited five-year-old on her hands was something my mother could well have done without.

I have an interesting note dated 15th March 1938, written in my father's hand but rubber-stamped with a swastika. It states that a search was undertaken at the home and chambers of my father and with the exception of three pistols which were freely handed over, nothing was found other than clients' matters. There was also an officer's sword, which my father was allowed to retain. The note refers to him as being a former officer, although his commission was not actually withdrawn until 10th June 1938. I can't help wondering whether the search was as peaceful as the note implies.

From other information it appears that on 15th March my parents were robbed of several items of valuable jewellery, but it is not clear whether this took place at home or at the Café Herrenhof. I am inclined to think it was at the café as my father names a waiter, Fritz Kornherr, a closet Nazi, as one of the culprits.

Theft, however, was not our family's only problem. Writing in 1955, my dad said that overnight his client base vanished, resulting in a total loss of income. At least one client refused to pay for work already done and invited him to sue for it. Other opponents took the opportunity to ask for the repayment of costs, some of which had been settled years previously. None of these matters could be treated lightly as the authorities to whom Dad should have been able to look for redress were not on his side. I have wondered why, if these included Jewish clients, they should have acted in this way, but it may be that because of their own loss of income, or as a result of exclusion from their own businesses, they were unable to continue to pay fees.

The perilous situation we were in can be illustrated by the following story.

My father owned a bathing hut in the resort town of Kritzendorf. It was a bigger building than one might expect from its title, as it had two rooms, a toilet, a veranda and quite a sizeable garden. In May 1938 Dad received a letter forbidding him as a Jew to go to Kritzendorf. The municipality also said they had valued the asset, which came out at one per cent of its acquisition price. They also required him to confirm that he freely transferred the property to the municipality. My dad complied.

Es wird bestätigt dass am 15. III. 38 in der Wohnung und Kanzlei des Dr. Franz Ferd. Popper, Wien, I. Raufensteingasse 8 eine Haussuchung vorgenommen wurde. Mit Ausnahme von 3 Pistolen die freiwillig abgegeben wurden wurden nur Klientengelder gefunden die belassen worden sind. Ebenso wurde ein Offizierssäbel dem Genannten als ehemaligem Offizier belassen.

Note referred to in text relating to raid

Another incident concerned the termination of the lease on our flat. The Jewish landlord, Mr Neumann, agreed with my dad that instead of the usual three months he would accept one month's notice of termination. The managing agent, who was not Jewish, did not demur when my father gave notice of termination to expire at the end of August 1938. However, in the middle of August he phoned my father and in a very rude manner demanded payment till 1st November, which was the original termination date. He threatened my dad with the Gestapo if he refused to pay. My dad, who had previously always found this man to be a jovial person, referred to the agreement, but the managing agent shouted that he did not care what arrangements Jewish people had made and payment had to be made until 1st November. For good measure, he also made other threats relating to various fixtures and fittings. Needless to say, my father again complied. I have wondered about this, but perhaps by this time Mr Neumann had been dispossessed and the additional payment was for the benefit of some non-Jewish person, possibly a Nazi.

The Nazis required all Jewish people who had assets above a minimum of RM[7] 5,000 to complete a return giving the details of their capital assets as of 27th April 1938. Mutti's return disclosed significant assets at the bank (over RM 11, 000), which depending on inflation and rates of exchange would be at least £40,000 today[8]. Despite trying very hard, I have not been able to trace such a return for my dad. Perhaps his capital assets were below the threshold and everything was in Mutti's name, but I think it is a bit odd.

The archives in Jerusalem have sent me a very interesting document addressed to the IKG which my father completed on 14th May 1938. He lists his occupation as *wine expert, gardener, beekeeper and doctor of law*. My paternal grandfather had been a wine merchant, which may explain why Dad considered himself a wine expert. He says that he wanted to be a gardener and beekeeper. He lists the countries to which he would like to travel as Australia, Canada, Argentina, Uruguay and New Zealand, and says he has no income but some cash. I can remember him once saying that he had managed to get at least some money back from the Nazis on the grounds that it was clients' money. From the way he said it I imagine that at least some of this money was actually his.

Nazi practice was to block Jewish bank accounts, but Mutti does not

---

7   Reichsmark, the currency after annexation.
8   January 2018

say in her declaration that this had happened to her. I have to assume that her money went towards living expenses and the costs of emigration, but by the time we were ready to leave my parents were unable to pay the amount required to enable them to take their Persian carpets abroad. I think it is safe to say that by the time we left, except for a minimal amount of cash which was allowed to be taken abroad, our money had all gone or ceased to be available to us.

Just before we left, however, my parents did manage to buy an Olivetti portable typewriter to mop up the small balance of the money they had which was above the export maximum. This proved to be a most worthwhile acquisition and innumerable letters were typed on it by Mutti, and later also by me. I still have the machine, but computers have displaced it.

Although in 1938 emigration was still possible, it was stressful and complicated as one had to obtain clearance from various authorities. It was also expensive, quite apart from any bribes which Mutti said had to be paid. Most relate to her parents, including a payment to an SA man who was threatening Omama (Grandma) with imprisonment. This threat had to be taken seriously as this man had been present when Opapa was arrested. There is more about this later in the book.

Our Olivetti typewriter

August must have been very tense. The tax clearances were time limited and due to expire on 15th August 1938. As we did not leave until the 27th that date would not have been any good, but fortunately my parents managed to get it extended twice, once to the 25th and the second time to the 31st. I think one can imagine the stress this must have caused; however, as far as I know neither of my parents was physically hurt or imprisoned. Many others had worse experiences, including Uncle Hans and Opapa. Both were imprisoned and Uncle Hans was assaulted. Even in these circumstances, we were the lucky ones.

For reasons which I do not know, we did not go to any of the countries my father had originally listed, but to Cyprus, a British Crown Colony. My father had visited it in the mid-'30s when he had gone on a holiday to Palestine. He presumably obtained a tourist visa as we would not get our permanent residence until sometime after we had been in Cyprus. We were to become genuine refugees.

My father knew he would not be able to practise law. He must have gone off the idea of being a beekeeper or a gardener too. Perhaps my parents thought that people ate sweets everywhere, so he and Mutti had a few lessons in sweet-making before leaving Vienna. I can remember a man coming to the flat to teach them, and I can also recall some kind of chocolate truffles cooling in the bath.

It is only fair to say that, notwithstanding all the problems and costs, we did not in fact leave Vienna destitute, though I think my father felt as if he was. This is understandable as he had to flee for his life, give up his home, lose his professional career and try to settle in a strange land. My parents had limited cash resources but they still owned valuable jewellery, and in addition to the four large trunks which would accompany us (and which weighed 241 kilograms) they were able to arrange for a four-square-metre container to be packed and forwarded to us in Cyprus. There must have been a hiccup with this too because Mutti records that Opapa had to pay a bribe to get the tax clearance extended to enable the container to leave Austria.

Everything had to be listed in detail. It would be tedious to set this out, but by way of example the list included three beds, lots of bedding and four chandeliers. I can remember playing with crystal in Cyprus, and I assume this came from one or other of the chandeliers. We also seem to have had an incredible amount of clothing. For example, there were twelve nighties, six sets of flannel pyjamas and ten sets of thin pyjamas for the children! By way of contrast, one doll, crayons and paper, and my scooter were also listed. The list of adult possessions included my dad's officer's sword, one tube of shaving cream and thirty-four shirts! Why on earth did we need so many clothes?

Shortly before our departure my father, in common with many others, decided that it would be wise to have us baptised. Historically this had been a way for Jewish people to become assimilated and avoid persecution, but it would not have worked with the Nazis.

I do not remember my baptism, but when, years later, I wanted to be baptised in East Africa, my father told me that I already had been, but he did not have the certificate as the Nazis were arresting people who went to collect them. Nor do I recall ever being told which church or denomination I had been baptised in. However, in March 2004 I came across the email address of Christ Church, which is the Anglican church in Vienna. Entirely on the off chance, I wrote and asked if they had the baptismal registers for 1938. To my amazement, not only did they have them, but they found entries not only for me but also for Mutti, Dad and Lisa. We were all baptised on 4th August 1938.

I understand that in the period March to September 1938 more than 1,800 people were baptised at Christ Church. Apparently this is a far higher number than at other Protestant churches in Vienna. It may be that people saw the Anglican church as giving them a better chance, or perhaps the priest in charge was more willing to try and help.

The priest who baptised us was the Rev. Frederick Collard. His predecessor, Hugh Grimes, had been officially appointed as chaplain and so had diplomatic immunity, but Rev. Collard did not and was arrested on 16th August and released on the 18th. I was told he was deeply shaken by his interrogation, but nevertheless carried on with a further 870 baptisms until 15th September 1938, when it all came to an abrupt end. Rev. Collard had only been ordained in 1936, and was in his mid-sixties.

Finding out about the baptism was not only very exciting for me, but also, I think, for Mr Christopher Wentworth Stanley, an English member of the congregation who, together with others, had done a lot of research into this period.[9]

---

9   On 8th August 2011, BBC Radio 4 broadcast a documentary about this, to which I contributed.

In addition to all the emigration preparations and no doubt the goodbyes, Mutti and Daddy were anxious to prepare us for the journey. The strategy my dad adopted was to tell us stories of an exciting day when he would announce that we were off to Kritzendorf. In reality my parents had no intention of going there, but this claim would enable him to get us onto the train and away with no difficulty. We used to climb into bed with him to hear the story and it was all very exciting.

On 26th August my parents paid off the rent and also made a payment for gas, electricity and the telephone. Someone named Maria Bader was paid off till that date, and she signed a receipt which Mutti had prepared for her. I do not know if she was a maid, a nanny or even a cook, but it is surprising that despite everything we had continued to have an employee until one day before we left. It is perhaps equally surprising that I still have the receipts for these payments.

On 27th August 1938 we boarded a train for Trieste in Italy. Mutti gave us chocolates called *Katzenzungen* (cats' tongues) to keep us quiet while the emigration formalities were dealt with on the train. It must have been a very tense time indeed. I have the vaguest of recollections of something happening but did not, of course, understand what was going on. It would not surprise me if we were given a small dose of a barbiturate so that we would sleep while we travelled through the night towards Italy and safety.

When I awoke in the morning and caught a glimpse of the sea, I was promptly sick. In Trieste I can picture myself in an enormous garden café or restaurant. It probably was not that grand, but to my eyes it looked wonderful.

Most of my journey to Cyprus is forgotten. We travelled with an Italian shipping line on a ship perhaps appropriately named *Gerusalemme*, i.e. Jerusalem. All I can remember is taking chocolate-flavoured calcium tablets which came in little tin containers and were known as Calcium Sandoz.

On 3rd September 1938 we arrived in Larnaca, Cyprus. A new life was about to begin.

On the way to Larnaca

4

Grandparents, Uncle Hans and the Café Herrenhof

Here I would like to interrupt my story and write something more about my maternal grandparents and uncle, and what became of the Café Herrenhof.

Albert Waldmann – or Bela as he was always known, but Opapa to me – was born in Boesing, Hungary on the 18th September 1870. He left school at thirteen with a good report. In 1888 he was apprenticed to a firm of sculptors, and again was given a glowing report. He married Omama on 2nd May 1897.

My grandmother Amalie Klug, also known as Malvine, was born in Sered, Slovakia on 29th December 1874. I know nothing of Omama's early life but I was told that she had a corset shop at some point.

In December 1914 at Herrengasse 10 Vienna I, the Café Herrenhof was founded by Opapa and his brother-in-law Marcus Klug. Their wives, Omama Amalie and Therese, were also involved.

The First World War would, I presume, have been a difficult time to run a successful café-restaurant, particularly towards the end when, among other things, food was scarce in Austria. However, these shortages must have been exploited for Omama was a good cook and knew that people were hungry.

Opapa and Uncle Marcus were innovative, and after the war got the first Cossack group which visited Vienna to play at the café. This was a

Bela Waldmann 1930

resounding success and the café prospered. I was told that Billy the Kid also appeared there when he toured Europe.

The café was a large establishment divided into several rooms and capable of seating about one thousand people. There was dancing in the ballroom in winter, and jazz music was played in one of the large coffee rooms. It was frequented by literati, and I was told that guests included Franz Werfel, Sigmund Freud and no doubt many other notable figures.

Friedrich Torberg, in his book[10] describes the Herrenhof as *the centre of Vienna's literary and intellectual life*.

In the mid-'30s renovation work was undertaken, and much of the design work was done by Mutti's only brother, Uncle Hans.

Opapa also co-owned the Café Josefstadt with his son Hans. There were in fact four café-restaurants owned by the Waldmann family (Herrenhof, Josefstadt, Schottentor and Bristol), and in addition Uncle Hans' parents-in-law Philip and Helene Steiner owned The Steiner.

Photographs taken in the mid-'30s give some idea of how the Café Herrenhof looked:

Frontage of Café Herrenhof 1937

10 Tante Jolesch or The Decline of the West in Anecdotes. ISBN 978-1-57241-149-4

Café Herrenhof *Grosse Saal* (Large Hall)

Café Herrenhof *Tanz Saal* (Dance Floor)

In the spring of 1938 my grandparents were well off, and my grandfather would no doubt have been proud of the café. This view seems to have been shared even by the Nazis, and by way of example one official[11] described it as "an internationally known and luxuriously furnished café." This is not to say that there was no need for repair or renovation; for example, the heating installation.

On 15th March, just three days after the Nazi annexation, the owners were summoned to attend a meeting at the Café Herrenhof. Opapa was ill, so Omama went as his representative. My dad attended as their lawyer, and Mutti was there as well. One of the Nazi ringleaders who met them turned out to be a long-standing employee, Fritz Kornherr, a closet Nazi, as the party had been illegal prior to the annexation. Threats were issued and they were searched allegedly for weapons, but in reality valuable items of jewellery and cash were stolen. The family were forbidden on pain of death or concentration camp to enter the premises. Instead the café would be run by the said Nazi waiter.

A couple of days later, a group of Nazis also called at the Café Josefstadt and a similar order was given.

The Nazis were anxious to get Opapa to agree to the sale of the Café Herrenhof, and events climaxed on 24th–25th April 1938 when the owners and other family members were again summoned to the café. Uncle Hans had been in hiding, but was going home that night. He noticed four Nazis and tried to run away, but stopped when they threatened to shoot him. He was taken to the Café Herrenhof where he and Uncle Marcus were subjected to indignities before a crowd of onlookers. He was then held and hit in the face, breaking his nose, following which he was paraded around the assembled relatives, care being taken that his parents should see him. Finally he was led into the office where he was made to sign a sale agreement for the Café Josefstadt for a nominal amount. He was told to attend at a lawyer's office the next day to finalise the legalities.

Ironically, the department dealing with the acquisition of Jewish property later ordered that the sale price for the Café Josefstadt be increased; an academic exercise as far as Uncle Hans was concerned, as he saw none of the money.

---

11 *Reichtreuhaender fuer Arbeit* (trustee for work).

The next day, following a search at his home and the removal of some items of value, Uncle Hans was arrested, taken to the Gestapo headquarters and questioned for hours, but they were unable to pin anything on him. He was nevertheless sent to prison. He was searched and for a couple of days did not eat anything, partly because the soup was inedible and partly because he could not properly swallow because of his injuries. He was then sent to hospital for a few days before being returned to prison and held in Cell 164. He was subjected to two further interrogations by the Gestapo but eventually released on the 9th June 1938, having agreed to leave Austria.

On 25th April Opapa and Uncle Marcus were also arrested, ostensibly for activities against the state. The true reason was, of course, to obtain their consent to dispose of the Café Herrenhof. The Nazis achieved this objective as Opapa and Uncle Marcus agreed to sell the business at a ridiculous price. They signed the document three days after their arrest. The document is interesting as in their own hand they have written that they have agreed to the sale without duress and of their own free will. Bearing in mind they were in prison, one can draw one's own conclusions as to the truth of this. This sale did not, in fact, proceed.

They were released on 7th June 1938 and expelled from Austria, but it proved extremely difficult to leave and Opapa and Omama only just managed it before the war began. Marcus and Therese also got out of Austria, but only made it to Yugoslavia where they were murdered after the Nazi occupation of that country.[12]

Following his release Opapa completed a form indicating a wish to sell, but there proved to be endless complications. It was not until 31st March 1939 that a contract (*Gedaechtnisprotokoll*) for the sale of the Café Herrenhof to the Gewerbebund der Stadt Wien (Vienna Trade Federation) was completed. My understanding is that Opapa did not know its content or any of the details, but had to agree to it. The valuation was only a fraction of what he thought the business was worth, and as far as he was concerned was an entirely arbitrary number. From this low figure various deductions were made, and the small balance remaining was not handed over but put in a blocked account.

---

12   Editors note: It is thought they were part of the Kladovo transport. The tragic story of this group of escapees, their journey and eventual murder is told in the book by Alisa Douer: Kladovo Escape to Palestine published by Mandelbaum Vienna ISBN 3-85476-044-2

I do not know how much Opapa knew of what was happening behind the scenes, but he wrote at least three letters commenting on his parlous financial position and asking that the sale be finalised so that he could settle his affairs and leave. It took, however, until August 1939 before he at last obtained his exit clearance, which was time-limited. At a meeting on 8th August 1939 it was agreed that the blocked balance should be released, but it seems that only a small part was released prior to his departure.

My grandparents left Vienna in August 1939 and arrived in Cyprus on the last boat from Italy prior to the commencement of the war on 3rd September 1939. They must have been so relieved to have got out, as things had been getting worse for Jews. On 10th November 1938 Kristallnacht occurred when most of the synagogues in Vienna were destroyed and many Jewish properties were also vandalised and ransacked.

In July 1939 Omama had to hand over several items to the Dorotheum, a large auction house and pawnbroker which still exists today. The valuations for the smaller items were paid out to Omama.

A more valuable item which was handed in was one earring. Mutti describes it as having two brilliant cut diamonds, one 2.2 carats and the other 0.5. Omama got nothing for this as it was sent to Berlin for valuation. It is intriguing to speculate why she only had one earring. However, it turns out that her sister-in-law Therese had what may have been the other one, though the Dorotheum sized this one at only 1.74 carats. Perhaps the pair of earrings were so expensive that they decided to share the cost and borrow each other's when they wanted to wear them.

The Austrian State Archives have sent me a number of documents which give some insight as to what was happening on the Nazi side. It seems that their objective was to deprive Jews of their wealth and assets whilst making it look legitimate and rational. Some of the events that occurred would be almost comical if it were not for the fact that the situation was so sad.

The former waiter and Nazi Mr Kornherr was appointed to run the business. He festooned the premises with swastikas and excluded Jewish customers from the establishment. He had, however, overlooked German racial legislation, and because a sale had not yet taken place it was still legally a Jewish café. On 4th April 1938 a note was sent out stating that Jewish establishments, even if they contained Nazi cells, were not allowed to display swastikas. Mr Kornherr did not initially comply and was threatened with proceedings under the 1935 Nuremberg laws. Some of his Aryan[13] customers now avoided the place, and so the Nazis succeeded within weeks in effectively ruining what had been a prosperous business.

Various offers to purchase were made including one from Mr Kornherr and also one from the head waiter Mr Albert Kainz, but these offers were withdrawn on 22nd June 1938. The very next day, Mrs Anna Ortner from the competitor Central Café wrote a letter to the deputy mayor noting that the Café Herrenhof was to close down (a fact apparently unknown at the time to Mr Kornherr). She suggested exchanging her café for the Café Herrenhof, but nothing seems to have come of this.

It did not take long before Mr Kornherr was made aware that his tenure was coming to an end, that the staff would lose their jobs and that the business would be liquidated. There are letters appealing against the decision, but in the end Mr Kornherr was threatened with dismissal if he did not implement the order to close. It seems he was replaced on 2nd July 1938.

The new administrator complained that it had taken weeks to get the swastika flags removed and when he took over there were still people with Nazi insignia and uniform in the café. The business was closed on 7th July. The liquidation was implemented so quickly that there were complaints that the staff, the majority of who were not Jewish, were dismissed without proper notice. Opapa must have been aware of this because he refers to the closure in an asset declaration which he prepared.

Mr Kornherr had not had a very successful run with the Nazi authorities. In less than four months he was threatened with prosecution, dismissal, required to run the business as a Jewish café, and finally ordered to close the Café Herrenhof. To cap it all, he was replaced just prior to the closure – perhaps not the events which he had expected.[14]

After closure, a valuation was ordered. This was a liquidation valuation which, after correcting a small error, was the basis for the figure in the contract which Opapa agreed to in March 1939. It is therefore of interest because it explains how the starting sale figure was arrived at as far as the

---

13 I am using this term here and elsewhere as it was in common usage at the time for non-Jewish people.

14 According to documents I have seen, he enlisted in March 1940 and was declared missing on 4th February 1943.

Nazis were concerned. It does not, however, explain how the further deductions were calculated.

In a note written by an unknown writer (but bearing a Nazi roundel), it is candidly admitted that the valuations were based on a break-up value from which debts had to be deducted so that for practical purposes, next to nothing remained for the true owners. Incidentally, prior to the Nazi annexation I understand the business had no significant debts, so the deductions were either fictitious or occurred after Opapa was excluded from running the business.

Not content with one valuation, the Nazis obtained another. This one is of even greater interest because among other things it values the business prior to the annexation at AS (Austrian Schillings) 400,000. Opapa thought it was worth AS 450,000 plus stock and cash in hand. The valuer notes that a liquidation valuation would be much lower. He was right, as the figure in the sales document after deductions, whether legitimate or not, left a notional amount for the owners of AS 13,511, which is 3.4% of what the valuer said the business had been worth before it was destroyed by the Nazi annexation.[15]

The Trade Federation of Vienna must have been enraged when the order to close was made on 7th July 1938, and obtained an injunction to suspend or cancel it. This must have come as a shock for Mrs Ortner. She wrote letters complaining and pleading for help, but these seemed to have fallen on deaf ears as on 30th August the Trade Federation acquired the Café Herrenhof and reopened part of it on 1st October, but with permission to trade for one year only.

There was further activity, as on 13th June 1939 it was agreed in principle that Mrs Ortner would rent the premises and transfer the Central Café licence to it. This was the second attempt to substitute the Café Herrenhof for the Central. Things did not run smoothly for her as she had financial problems. It also became known that her son, a member of the Nazi Party, had acquired another Jewish café, and it was presumably not allowed for one family to own two Jewish businesses.

On 2nd August 1939 the same person whose initial closure order on the Café Herrenhof had been overturned again ordered that it be closed immediately. On the very next day a *Staatskommisar* overruled this order.

---

15   Note that some of the documents refer to Reichsmarks. I have converted these to AS at the appropriate rate of AS 1.5 = RM 1.

Another setback for the former deputy mayor! Trading was authorised to continue to the end of September.

On 6th October negotiations again came to an end, and there seems to be a suggestion that the Café Herrenhof closed, but it is difficult to work out exactly what happened.

On 29th November 1940 the former head waiter Mr Albert Kainz acquired the Café Herrenhof excluding the dance hall for RM 41,000 (AS 61,500). This is even less than the liquidation valuation used in the contract for sale. He ran it during the war years.

When the war ended Opapa and Omama were in Africa, but they returned to Cyprus in the spring of 1946, about a year before us. Uncle Marcus (Klug) and his wife Therese were dead but their two daughters were alive, Annie in Palestine and Grete in London.

In the autumn of 1946 Mr Albert Kainz somehow got in touch with Opapa. Mr Kainz had been a trusted employee and head waiter, and Opapa had thought highly of him prior to the annexation. Mr Kainz indicated that he was willing to return the Café Herrenhof, but wanted to retain a stake. At this time the café had been requisitioned as a Russian officers' mess.

I wish I could say that negotiations went like clockwork, but sadly that is not the case. They were very difficult, not least because letters went astray. The only practical, speedy way of communicating was by telegram. This was very expensive, though if sent at night and restricted to twenty-four words or less it was a little cheaper. Great ingenuity was needed to keep the message short and yet clear. The telegrams had to be taken to the main post office in Nicosia for transmission, and this task sometimes fell to me.

Mr Kainz's proposal was initially not favourably received, but after an enormous amount of correspondence all parties agreed that he would have a 20% stake. With difficulty a contract was drawn up and completed in early 1949. By this time the dance hall had also been returned, so the Café Herrenhof was, as far as the premises were concerned, intact once more.

Despite their age, Opapa and Omama wanted to return to Vienna and take over or at least participate in running the business. It all came to nothing because Omama died on 26th August 1950. Opapa was devoted to her, and shortly after her death returned to his son who still lived in Africa.

The Russians vacated the premises in late 1948 or early 1949. Mr

Kainz worked hard and the Café Herrenhof reopened for business in March 1949.

Sadly, the Café Herrenhof did not do that well and it was a struggle from the word go. Opapa was sure that something was not right, particularly when he saw that the monthly accounts contained items which he was not happy with. In 1953 he decided to transfer his 40% stake to Mutti, who was very pleased, but in truth it was a poisoned chalice that was unwittingly handed over.

By this time Grete[16] was back in Vienna, working in the café. She had remarried, a lawyer named Max Rappaport. Unfortunately he was not an easy person to negotiate with and things went from bad to worse. Correspondence, which now was mainly with Grete and Max, was polite but more or less acrimonious.

My dad dictated sometimes very lengthy letters for Mutti, who typed them on the Olivetti typewriter which had travelled with us from Vienna. She must have been an accurate typist to be able to do this – no computers or spellcheckers in those days!

In 1956 Dad, Mutti and I went to Vienna for the first time since we left in 1938. My dad by this time was very ill. Whilst there we ate at the Café Herrenhof, and I was fortunate to be able to see it in its original size. To my untutored eyes it looked lovely. If there was any personal animosity I did not notice it. I then left for my first visit to England, but had to return to Vienna as my dad died there on 23rd August 1956. Later that year Mutti and I returned to Cyprus.

Mutti was convinced that the café was worth AS 1,000,000, making her share AS 400,000. I think she saw this as a net sum, but on reflection she may not have been correct in this. In October 1958 Mutti withdrew from the partnership, and in September 1959 she commenced legal proceedings. In December of that year she received an offer of AS 200,000 which her lawyer Dr Pranter turned down – in the event, a bad mistake. A court-appointed valuer valued her interest at practically nothing, and it was obvious that Mutti would now lose the case.

Surprisingly, the opponents, saying this was for ethical reasons, proposed a couple of compromises. One of these was that Mutti

---

16 Grete, daughter of the former co-owner Marcus Klug.

would receive a 20% share of the proceeds of any disposals less various deductions. This was better than nothing, and so she agreed. In June 1961 an offer of AS 1,000,000 was made for the Café Herrenhof. Mutti felt vindicated, and felt that the court valuer had got his figures wrong.

The opponents produced a computation which did start off with the above sum. However, after various deductions Mutti received net AS 70,000; about £1,000 at that time. This was about 35% of the offer her lawyer had turned down, and about 17.5% of what she had hoped for initially. Right or wrong, it is now water under the bridge and best left in peace.

For completeness, she did receive a further sum of AS 10,220, being 20% of a compensation payment relating to the Russian use of the premises after the war. Mutti felt, I think rightly, that she should have received 40% of this compensation as it related to events prior to the dissolution, but there was nothing she could do about it. By the time she paid her lawyer's fees Mutti received in England a sum of somewhat less than £500.

I was really pleased when it was all over. It had created a huge amount of work for Dad and Mutti, with much stress and upset. It is a shame that it ended so disappointingly for her. I had no interest in the Café Herrenhof at the time. If I had had my way in the late '50s and early '60s, we would have abandoned it altogether.

Over the years feelings mellowed, and in 1979 when Mutti and I went to Vienna we visited Grete in her flat in the Rotenturmstrasse overlooking the cathedral. By this time Max had died and Grete was very ill, still smoking and painfully thin. I remember that following our flight to Vienna I had a very bad earache and I think Mutti did too, but no doubt she and Grete managed to reminisce as we drank coffee together.

A few years later I discovered that there was a small bistro, still called the Café Herrenhof, in a small front section of the original café. Lisa and I ate there when we visited Vienna, and so did my daughter Susan when she took me there for my seventieth birthday. We enjoyed the food as they still knew how to cook. On 18th August 2006 it closed for good. The whole building has been taken over and converted into a large, luxurious hotel, The Herrenhof.

You may wonder how it is that I know anything about the Café Herrenhof. In 2003 Austria set up a compensation fund called the

General Settlement Fund and Lisa and I put in a claim, including one for the Café Herrenhof. We did a lot of work researching it. By the time a decision was reached in 2008 Lisa had died, and as far as the Café Herrenhof was concerned the claim was rejected.

5

Cyprus

Now to return to my story. It must have been a strange and daunting experience for my parents to arrive in Larnaca, Cyprus on 3rd September 1938 with two small children who only spoke German. Their own language skills were limited and they had no jobs, little money, and were faced with a significant change in status. Quite apart from this were their anxieties about the people left behind in Austria.

Landing in Larnaca was by lighter onto a long pier as the liners had to anchor out at sea. I remember the pier because once when walking along it my foot got stuck and I cried as I thought I would not be able to free myself. Tears were also shed when I realised that my teddy had been lost, and no doubt on many other occasions too.

Larnaca is close to a salt lake where at times flamingos can be seen. On a road to the lake stands the Tekke, an Islamic holy place where the prophet Mohammed's aunt was buried. Surrounded by gardens, it is an oasis in an otherwise dry landscape. More centrally in the old part of the town there is a large church dedicated to St. Lazarus.

Near the pier there was a promenade which was very popular with locals who, in the cool of the evening, enjoyed walking along it, and no doubt so did we. The promenade was fronted by coffee shops and hotels and my parents and other refugees used to meet to drink coffee and talk; the names Sun Hall and Four Lanterns Hotel spring to mind. In that sense Cyprus was a café-orientated society just as Vienna had been. I must have been aware that momentous things were happening as I wanted to listen to the adults, but this was frowned on.

Our first home was rented accommodation in Kimon Street. Tante Edith, Uncle Hans and their daughter Franzi, left Austria on 16th September 1938, and on their arrival in Cyprus, joined us there.

I assume that we entered Cyprus with a tourist visa, and suspect it would have been time-limited and contained employment restrictions. Consequently, one of the first and most important tasks was to obtain permanent resident status. This would give us security and enable my parents to work. It would also enable them to sponsor Opapa and Omama to come to Cyprus. One had to have a certain amount of cash to be eligible for permanent resident status, and Mutti sold jewellery to help pay for it. It was granted on 21st December.

My father applied for Opapa and Omama to join us and permission was granted on 19th January 1939. It still took till August before they were able to leave Vienna. Sadly, Tante Edith's parents did not survive the war. Both were sent to the Theresienstadt ghetto, where her father died. Her mother survived until almost the end of the war, when she was deported to Auschwitz on the last transport to leave the ghetto.

On 1st December 1938 we were issued with German passports in lieu of our Austrian ones. My parents probably were not too happy about this but they had no choice in the matter.

Cyprus in those days was cheap. In my head is a figure of £4 per month for food and possibly other expenses for our family. My parents did not enjoy some of the local food, like halloumi and the Cypriot round bread loaves. More to our taste was the delicious continental bread, which for a time my dad was able to obtain from the Italian liners.

Commencing their little business, my parents made agar-agar orange and lemon slices. Agar-agar is an expensive, flavourless, transparent gelling agent made from seaweed. It can be mixed with boiled sugar solution, coloured and flavoured as required.

The orange and lemon slices were complicated to make. Boiled sugar with agar-agar was poured into cylinders to make the orange centres. To make the 'pith' the solution was whitened, I think with egg white, and then poured onto a tray in a thin layer and allowed to set. For the 'peel', clear, coloured jelly was set in trays. The jelly became very sticky when set. Having first taken the central core out of its mould, it would be carefully rolled over the 'pith' jelly and then over the 'peel' jelly, the difficulty being to get the edges to join neatly. The completed cylinders would be sliced and usually cut in half to make semicircles. These were then tossed in granulated sugar, packed neatly in presentation boxes and sold.

Meanwhile, both Lisa and I developed spots and boils. Lisa contracted paratyphoid too, and so was quite ill for a time.

When health permitted we attended the American Academy, which was a Christian mission school run by the Reformed Presbyterians from the USA. The student body was multi-ethnic and tuition was in English. Apparently, after sitting silently in class for about six months we could speak English. I remember nothing else about our education save singing songs on a school outing. The school magazine, the *American Herald*, dated 20th December 1938, featured us dressed identically, together with four other sets of twins, all Armenian.

Sometime in 1939, probably in the spring, we left Larnaca and moved to Platres, a resort in the Troodos mountain range. Here Lisa and I finally got rid of our boils!

Platres was a delightful village set high up in the Troodos mountains, and was a popular tourist resort. My parents rented a property and opened a little coffee shop. On some adjoining land my father had a play area fashioned. I remember playing there with some crystal from a chandelier which we had brought with us from Vienna. I am sure other children must have played there too.

Mutti baked cakes for the café. These were so good that they were often sold whole before they could be cut. I liked being with her when she baked because I wanted to lick the cake mix from the mixing bowls. Pickings were meagre as Mutti thought that raw flour was bad for me! I also pleaded for salami when she made sandwiches but usually had to be satisfied with the skin, which at least could be scraped clean with my teeth and sucked for flavour.

My dad made homemade ice cream in a hand churn, which must have been heavy work. Crushed ice sprinkled with salt was used to lower the temperature of the mix so that the ice cream could form. My interest, I imagine, again lay in licking the emptied container and mixing paddle.

One of the highlights for my mother must have been the arrival of her parents in Platres. They left Vienna on 13th August 1939, embarking on the last passenger ship to leave Trieste in Italy for Cyprus before the outbreak of the war. I imagine there were many hugs and kisses that evening, and immense relief.

Lisa and I had opportunities to go riding. Once my horse bolted and I could not stop it. I was very scared, but the owner managed to catch it and nothing happened to me. Another time I was on a donkey with Lisa and the saddle slipped sideways. I was in front and could see the stony ground approaching, so to pre-empt a fall I threw myself off before we reached the stones. Unfortunately I did not tell Lisa of my plan and she fell off unexpectedly. I was not popular.

Once I was taken to a Jewish prayer meeting in someone's home, possibly taking place after the declaration of war. I may have been taken along to make up male numbers as there is a stipulated minimum, but I doubt I would have counted as I was only seven at the time. Although my dad was not an observant Jew he could read Hebrew and so would have been able to participate, but of course I did not understand a thing.

Looking back now, I think that summer must have been almost idyllic for us children. All good things come to an end however, and when the season ended we returned to the plains, this time to Nicosia.

Nicosia was the capital of Cyprus. It had been a moated, walled city, but had begun to outgrow the walls. As in the rest of Cyprus, the bulk of its population was Greek but there were a sizeable number of Turks and also quite a few Armenians. Nearly everyone spoke Greek and at some point I too became fluent in it without formal teaching. Different ethnic groups tended to live together in their own sectors. The Armenians lived mainly in the Turkish Muslim sector. This seems surprising as they were Christian and many of them had fled to Cyprus from Turkey. Perhaps it was easier to settle in a location where at least they understood the language.

Our rented accommodation was at 44A Victoria Street, a lovely large older house in the Turkish/Armenian area. We shared the house with my grandparents and another refugee family who had one son a little older than us. Immediately opposite the house was a small mosque. Five times a day the muezzin call to prayer echoed from its one minaret.

Behind the house was an enclosed yard or garden where we kept two chickens called Hansel and Gretel. Despite their names, I think they were both female. Their intended destiny was probably the table, but things did not work out that way as we could not bear to be parted from them. I fear that at some point they did meet a sticky end, perhaps when we left Nicosia.

Schooling mattered, and although there was an American Academy close by my parents decided to send us to St. Joseph's, a Roman Catholic convent school located at the far end of Victoria Street. Perhaps they thought it was safer for us to get there as it was on the same side of the road as our house. The school was primarily for girls, but they took small boys. Tuition was in French, but neither then nor later did I master that language.

On the way to and from school there was a small grocery that sold sweets and other goodies. I regret to have to say that at times I pinched some of these without being caught. Why I should want to do this when my parents made sweets is a puzzle.

One day I fell over while carrying a milk bottle and cut the palm of my right hand quite badly. Treatment involved disinfecting it with iodine, so as you can imagine, I screamed. However, the treatment worked and my hand healed up beautifully without any stitches.

Another time as I was walking into the yard, Omama stopped me, looked at my eyes and decided that they were yellow. A diagnosis of jaundice was made. I was treated with bed rest and a high carbohydrate diet with exclusion of protein and fats as far as possible. Huge quantities of cherry compote spring to mind. To ameliorate my situation, I was allowed to use our His Master's Voice wind-up gramophone. I remember playing March Militaire by Schubert over and over again. I also amused myself by playing with my clockwork train. It was nothing grand but, no doubt supplemented by childhood imagination, it gave me hours of enjoyment.

Lisa, who was more industrious than I, learned to read German with Opapa as her teacher. He was also an exceedingly good chess player and I assume he taught me to play, but I did not excel at the game.

My parents were again making sweets. There was a large Armenian family living close by and I believe some of them helped with this work. When I visited their home I was surprised to see that they all seemed to share a large, dormitory-like bedroom. The family were kind to me and sometimes took me along with them when they went to the Turkish baths. In those days I could not have minded the heat and enjoyed going.

One of my ambitions was to run around barefoot outside as I had seen others do. The opportunity came when someone was moving house and I said I would help to carry things. The road was so hot that it felt as if the soles of my feet were being burned! This cured me of that ambition.

Lisa had a friend called Dorothy Heald, the daughter of a German Jewish refugee family, and I tagged along. Dorothy's house had trees in the garden and she and Lisa had perfected a technique of hanging from the branches upside down. I was scared but was persuaded to try it on a promise that they would hold me. Having got me on the branch, however, they decided to let go and I fell on my head. I was not amused. The girls had also invented a language which I never mastered where words were prefixed with certain letters. I must have felt they were ganging up on me.

On 3rd June 1940 my father and other Jewish refugees from Austria and Germany were interned as enemy aliens, though I doubt that there would have been any Nazi sympathisers among them. This put an end to my parents' sweet-making activity. The internees were initially housed in the Central Prison in Nicosia, but were then moved to Prodromos and housed in the Hotel Berengaria overlooking the village. Berengaria was the name of the wife of King Richard the Lionheart, whom he had married in Cyprus while travelling on a Crusade. In a commanding position and quite out of proportion to the village itself, the Berengaria was considered in those days to be one of the best hotels on the island. Prodromos was reputed to be the highest village in Cyprus and is beautifully located with an excellent climate, and so the transfer was a very welcome exchange from the Central Prison in Nicosia.

We followed my dad and rented a property which was built into the side of the hill on the road from Prodromos to Platres. It had a veranda with lovely views overlooking the valley and the more distant mountains, and was just a short walk from the hotel. At one end of the veranda there was a small enclosed space, which I claimed as my den, filled with bits of wood and other things boys have to play with. I was quite content. There were apple orchards alongside the road and I sometimes succumbed to temptation and picked an apple. Maybe I had been told not to, but anyway I felt guilty. Similarly, my wife Wendy recalls that when our son Geoffrey was small and saying his bedtime prayers, he once told her to "Tell God I did pick a pear", meaning he had helped himself to one without asking.

I think the internees must have been on their honour as I cannot remember fences or guards. In the mornings Lisa and I, together with other children, went to the hotel and sat in the grounds while my dad told us stories of the Greek war with Troy and the voyages of Ulysses.

One girl who we called Ulli loved the story of Achilles and wanted to hear the story of the "iron man" over and over again. It will be remembered that at birth Achilles was dipped in liquid which gave him an armour coating everywhere except his ankle where he had been held. This weak spot is still known as the Achilles tendon.

The adults trekked up to the hotel in the afternoons to be with the internees. There was a lovely terrace where one could take refreshments and I think at times listen to music.

Although the men were deprived of their liberty, as internment goes this probably was as good as it gets. On 30th October 1940 my dad was released subject to reporting regularly at a police station.

Following Dad's release, we returned to Nicosia. This time my parents rented accommodation in a Greek area quite a long way from Victoria Street. Chrysaliniotissa Street was so named because it contained an important Greek Orthodox church dedicated to the Virgin Mary. We lived at Number 9 and the church was quite close by. It may have been in this church that I used to kiss the icons with my Greek friends.

The house we rented was of single-storey construction. Its front door opened directly from the road onto a big hallway. On either side of the hall were two big rooms. The back of the hall opened onto a central enclosed garden with rooms around the sides. One would never have suspected how pleasant the house was by looking at it from the outside. Omama and Opapa did not move with us this time. They must have gone to live with their son who had found work at a mine in Polis, a town near Paphos.

My parents again started to make sweets, but they also had other culinary skills, the results of which we enjoyed. Cyprus is a wine-producing country and one of the wines is *Commandaria,* a dark red, sweet dessert wine that goes back to the Crusades. It was ridiculously cheap and sometimes we were allowed a little sip. Mutti also used to make a delicious sweet which we knew as *wine chaudeau* but is more easily recognised as sabayon. It was made with wine, egg yolk and sugar which was heated over a water bath while being actively whisked. We used to eat this with sponge cake, also made by my mother.

My father sometimes made a drink he called *Krambambouli,* and used to sing a German song about it. It was made by igniting spirit, such as brandy or a Cypriot clear spirit called *zivania,* both of which were cheap and plentiful. Over this was suspended a sugar lump balanced on a fork, which melted and dropped into the liquid. It was then ready to drink. Of course, we were only allowed a taste.

This time Lisa and I went to the local Greek school, where the boys and girls were segregated in adjoining buildings. I already spoke Greek but must have learned to read it too as I can still just about decipher printed Greek. Writing is another matter.

To recap, then, on our educational history to the age of nine. We spoke German at home. Our first three school years in Cyprus were spent in three different schools, each of which taught in a language foreign to us. Soon our education would be further significantly interrupted.

In the evenings we all walked to the police station near the Kyrenia Gate so that my father could register as required, and then across town to Metaxas (now called Eleftheria) Square. The attraction was a coffee shop where refugee families congregated.

Among the restrictions which applied to enemy aliens, as we were classed, was that we were prohibited from owning a radio, and it may be that the coffee shop provided a forum for obtaining and sharing news, whether accurate or not. Of course it was also an opportunity for socialising with German-speakers in those dark days. I used to love to sit and listen to the grown-up talk but my parents were very protective and so I tended to be excluded just when things got really interesting. Perhaps as a sop, I was occasionally treated to a stick of *souflakia* (kebab) from one of the mobile stalls on Metaxas Square. Cooked over charcoal, these were delicious.

As a precaution, zig-zag trenches had been dug in the now-dry moat outside the city walls to be used as air-raid shelters. There were several air-raid alarms but most of them did not develop into anything, and there was only one occasion when a bomb was dropped as I remember. At night if there was an alarm we used to be put to sleep under the table or bed. My dad also decided to have a small air-raid shelter constructed in our garden, but ours had a roof. It was great, except that all our neighbours thought so too. If an alarm sounded and the front door was not quickly shut, they would rush through the house and perhaps there would then not be room for us in it!

I was allowed to go out on my scooter, but not too far. One day I was bringing home some shopping and the alarm sounded. I rushed home and lost quite a bit of the shopping on the way. I am pretty certain that when we opened the front door after the all-clear sounded it had been picked up and stacked there for us. The Cypriot people were, and are, very friendly and hospitable.

The sweet business was about to be disrupted as events moved against us again. The Italians invaded Greece but without much success, and following the rejection of an ultimatum by the Greeks, the Germans invaded the mainland and also Crete.

It was my understanding that it was thought that Cyprus would be the next island on the invasion list, so the British government decided to evacuate the British expatriate wives and children and the Jewish refugees. With hindsight that proved unnecessary as the Germans never took Cyprus, but at the time we were very glad that action was being taken to protect us. The irony is that although we were considered enemy aliens, we were also treated as people in need of protection. I have always been grateful to the British government for their intervention.

I do not think we had much notice of the evacuation, and also we were only allowed to take what luggage we could carry. I carried the Olivetti typewriter, which I could only just manage.

Neither were we very skilful in ensuring that our other belongings were preserved. Apparently we sold what we could at knock-down prices but the rest was, I think, simply abandoned. I seem to recall that we just opened the doors and let people help themselves when we left. So now all we owned was what we carried.

I will say now that when we returned to Cyprus after the war some people had kept our photographs and returned these to us. Mutti also saw her picture by Bo Yin Ra on someone's wall and it was given back to her. It may be that there were other items which we got back. Certainly Mutti had a Brussels lace tablecloth right up to the date of her death. I cannot believe that this would have been a priority item to take on an evacuation, so we must have recovered it on our return.

6

Uncle Hans and Family

Uncle Hans (on right) – with Bela Waldmann his father

Mutti's younger brother Johannes, or Uncle Hans as I knew him, arrived in Cyprus with his wife Aunt Edith and their daughter Franzi a short while after us. As mentioned earlier, he had had a rough time in Austria prior to his departure and his escape turned out to be no less dramatic.

Following his release from prison on 9th June 1938 he made preparations to leave, and on 25th July was about to sign the contract to transfer his flat to a couple who had made him a fair offer. On that very day a young woman wearing a large swastika called and insisted on looking around. A short while later he was informed on the phone that the flat had been allocated to her. The original purchasers were livid and wanted initially to go to court, but Uncle Hans persuaded them not to as he feared that he would end up in a concentration camp. They probably were not keen to take on the Nazi Party either. The assigned tenant paid a token sum for the furniture, but nothing for the lease.

Finally on 16th September my uncle and aunt were able to leave Austria, having been made to sign an undertaking renouncing their possessions and agreeing never to return. They were given money for a return ticket and RM 40 (RM 20 per person), plus a cheque for £60, which was essential for gaining admission to Cyprus. The return ticket was a fiction as far as the Nazis were concerned, but essential if entry into Cyprus was to be obtained.

Sometime prior to their departure a distant relative who lived in Bratislava, Czechoslovakia had come to Vienna to see them. On his return he took with him their jewellery, the idea being that they would collect it when they eventually were able to leave Austria.

However, by the time they were able to leave they were no longer allowed entry into Czechoslovakia, so they decided to get a boat along the Danube to Yugoslavia and from there journey on to Trieste. Presumably their relative intended to meet them in Yugoslavia, or perhaps they could have got into Czechoslovakia from there.

Things worked out rather differently than they had planned. When their ship docked at Vukovar, a loudspeaker announcement was made that Jewish passengers were to present themselves to the captain. They duly did so and were told that they could not be taken further but would have to return to Austria. That would have meant disaster because the Nazis saw the journey as one-way with no possibility for return.

It must have been known that Uncle Hans was short of money because other passengers had a whip-round to raise some extra funds for them. However, the Yugoslav authorities would not allow them to disembark.

Just as the boat was moving off, Uncle Hans decided that their only option was to jump off the ship onto the quay. He jumped first, holding his two-year-old daughter and shouting to Tante Edith to do likewise. By the time she jumped there was already clear water between the boat and the quay, but fortunately she managed it. The other passengers turned up trumps again and threw their belongings onto land for them. Probably fortunately for them, the boat continued to move away.

At least they were now on Yugoslavian soil, but as no one knew what to do next the police were called. Faced with a fait accompli, the Yugoslavian authorities behaved decently towards them and they were escorted by the police to a hotel for the night. As it was full, a maid was asked to vacate her own room for them.

One can imagine the state of panic the family was in. They did not know what was going to happen and more importantly were terrified that they would miss the boat at Trieste. Uncle Hans phoned Omama in Vienna and asked her to go to the steamship company Lloyd Triestino and request that the departure of the boat be delayed. Not only did the company agree to this, but apparently one of their employees was sent to look after them and travel to Trieste with them on the train. The boat had waited for them and sailed as soon as they had embarked. I have no idea whether they ever managed to collect the jewellery which was the raison d'être for travelling this route.

Once in Cyprus, they initially lived with us in Larnaca. Uncle Hans was an engineer and architect by profession, which is a practical occupation for a refugee, and in due course found a job in a mine in Polis.

After evacuation from Cyprus to East Africa he obtained a job with the railways in Tanganyika. On retirement he moved to London where he died on 1st November 1986. This was a hard blow for Tante Edith, but she continued to live on in London and died at the ripe old age of 102 on 29th June 2008. Her daughters[17] Franzi and Peggy – who was born in Tanzania – now have children and grandchildren of their own.

---

17 Franzi married Monty Howard and has two children, Helena and Judi. Peggy is now married to Michael Wilson and has one daughter, Joanna, with her first husband.

7

Evacuation: Cyprus to Palestine, and on to Tanganyika

And so back to the time of the evacuation.

On 11ᵗʰ June 1941 we travelled to Famagusta. There, together with many other families, we embarked on the *SS Hanna*, arriving in Haifa the next day. We learned later that the Germans had claimed that they had sunk our ship with us on board!

Haifa is an interesting city and an important port. It is built on Mount Carmel, a significant site in the Old Testament. It was there that the prophet Elijah defeated several hundred prophets of Baal by calling fire from Heaven to consume his sacrifice; something which they could not accomplish.[18]

Maybe because Haifa was a sea port, we were moved on to a camp near Tel Aviv. Men and women slept in separate dormitories. Lisa and I were with Mutti, but at some point during our stay some of the women complained that I was too old and as a consequence I was transferred to the men's section. I was very proud to receive this promotion.

Mutti used her interest in astrology to prepare horoscopes for some of the people who were keen to learn what the stars had in store for them. Others also claimed fortune-telling skills and one lady read my palm. I think I date my initial feelings of wanting to be to a doctor to her forecast, although now I do not hold with palmistry. However, in the situation in which we found ourselves such a suggestion would have been most welcome, for not only did it postulate survival, but also success.

---

18 1 Kings Ch. 18 V. 17–46.

At some point I was given a pocket Red Letter New Testament, probably by visiting Christian missionaries. Although I did not read it at the time, I kept it.

We moved out of the camp into a single ground-floor room in Tel Aviv, a large, modern city on the sea coast. Presumably there was a shared toilet and bathroom and, although I do not remember Mutti cooking, I imagine shared kitchen facilities. Often, if not every day, we used to go out to a restaurant (or perhaps it was some sort of soup kitchen) for lunch. I remember enjoying fruit soups and eating under a booth during the Feast of Tabernacles.

Our room had a small veranda with a stone or concrete wall which was an important play area for me. I used to run my one broken railway carriage up and down the wall, pretending it was a train. The rails were imaginary. I no doubt would have liked a complete railway set, but I think I was quite content.

In the same block there was a film studio. I was allowed to go in and watch while they cut and manipulated the film. Sadly these visits came to an end when I stepped on a live wire which stuck to my shoe until the current was switched off. Although that was not my fault and I was not hurt, I was not allowed into the studio again.

We enjoyed living on the coast and I have a lovely memory of my father taking Lisa and me by the hand and walking into the sea, where we jumped up and down through the large breakers. He also took us to a milk bar to drink buttermilk, which he had enjoyed in Austria but in Cyprus had not been available to him.

Adjacent to Tel Aviv was Jaffa, a very old city largely inhabited by Arabs at that time. I remember once going to eat in a restaurant there. My dad took a bite of a chilli which was unexpectedly hot. How my lips burned when I too had a taste! It caused quite a lot amusement to the local folk.

I must have had problems with my milk teeth because some of them were pulled or filled. I was very proud of my courage, but Lisa did not take kindly to seeing the dentist! My parents had the worst of it as they developed a gum disease which needed treatment and which I think led to the loss of most of their teeth. Poor Mutti used to walk about for a while with her hand in front of her mouth to hide the fact.

Because of the war we also had to try on gas masks as a precaution. I do not think I was quite as brave about this as I had been at the dentist, but at least I got mine on, which is more than Lisa did.

In Tel Aviv I discovered two types of chocolate spread: one hard and difficult to spread, and a more liquid one which I preferred. It was not easy to get and for us was expensive, so when some was bought it was eked out as much as possible, but even so, did not last long.

When I was nine Mutti decided that I should learn to read German, and soon made me read ten pages unsupervised each afternoon before I could play. It used to take me ages, and it was only later that I discovered that I was counting both sides as one page and so really reading twenty pages! Not only did I manage to read ordinary Roman lettering, but I somehow managed Gothic script as well. I never learnt to spell in any meaningful way. Lisa was always better than me at this – she could read and write German fluently.

Things could not always have gone smoothly at home as I can remember running away twice. I did not go far before turning back. Maybe I was more affected by the situation in which we found ourselves than I realised.

Soon we were on the move again. Did my parents know that we, together with several other refugee families, would be settled in Tanganyika?

On 25th November 1941 we travelled to Cairo by train across the Sinai desert. Part of this journey was at night and I can remember looking out at the desert scenery as I had heard there were jackals there. On arrival we were taken to the Luna Park Hotel near the centre of Cairo.

Among Mutti's papers I found a menu in French from the hotel, dated 1st December 1941. It is interesting because it sets out the table d'hôte dinner which consisted of:

Potage a la Portugaise
Riz a la Financiere
Sauce Tomate
Aubergine a L'Orientale
Pommes Boulangere
Salad Verte Pre
Creme Bavaroise aux Prunes
Cafe Moca

There does not seem to be an obvious fish dish on this menu, but I did eat a white fish dish there which was delicious.

My father was a smoker; mainly cigarettes, but also a pipe at times. Before we left Tel Aviv I had noticed the little ashtray that he used lying about unpacked. I could not bear to leave it behind, so picked it up and put it in my pocket and immediately forgot about it. Lying on the bed in the hotel room, Dad lit up a cigarette. He was looking around for an ashtray when I remembered that I had his little dish in my pocket. I took it out and gave it to him. He was thrilled by it, and so was I by his delight. It is only a small thing, but fixed in my memory.

In Cairo we were taken to the zoo. Oddly enough it is not the animals that I recall, but the paths inlaid with coloured stones like mosaics. Perhaps we were also taken to the Pyramids and Sphinx. Cairo was, of course, merely a staging post while we awaited our onward journey.

In due course we boarded a former passenger liner which was now used as a troop carrier. I have been told that we were on a separate deck to the troops and that there was a rule against fraternisation. Apparently, however, this did not stop a soldier falling in love with an attractive girl on our deck.

The ship sailed down the east coast of Africa where, on 17th December 1941, we would leave it in Dar es Salaam (which means Haven of Peace). Whilst on board we were given an apple a day which was always lovely as it came out of a cold store. I was also introduced to porridge, which I hated and resolutely refused to eat. However, in the end I was persuaded to get it down by eating a spoonful of porridge with a teaspoonful of sugar. Future breakfasts did not include porridge.

By this time I had made a special friend called Peter Hoffer and spent a lot of time playing with him and another boy called Paul Heim. One game involved hopping on one leg, folding our arms across our chests and pushing against the opponent with the intention of unbalancing him or sometimes even knocking him over. I liked the game as I tended to win, probably because I was heavier.

I know that there were other children on board including Lisa, Franzi, Ulli and Dorothy, but maybe because they were girls their activities do not feature in my memory. I have been told that I was considered a naughty boy, so perhaps I am lucky with my memory lapses!

Before the First World War the vast country of Tanganyika was a German colony. After that war it became mandated by the League of Nations to Great Britain so was not, strictly speaking, a colony, though I doubt that it made much practical difference to ordinary people. It now forms the continental part of Tanzania; the name being derived from its merger with Zanzibar Island.

The country was divided into administrative divisions which were run by provincial commissioners. The provinces were divided into districts, each of which had a district commissioner in charge. Dar es Salaam was the capital.

There were numerous tribal languages but Swahili was spoken by many people. It is supposed to be easy to learn, but I never mastered it. The black indigenous population was mainly Bantu, but around Arusha it was Masai. There were also small European and somewhat larger Asian communities. Many of the Asians had, I think, come over to work on construction projects. There was definite segregation between the races at that time; for instance, at railway stations there were separate toilets, and schools were firmly segregated.

There were two principal railway lines in the country. One ran from Dar es Salaam, bifurcating at Tabora with one branch going to Kigoma on Lake Tanganyika and the other to Mwanza on Lake Victoria. The second line was shorter and ran from Tanga, a port in the north of the country, to Arusha. It was important because it also connected to the Kenyan rail network.

On arrival in Dar es Salaam instructions were given to proceed by train to Tabora, about seven hundred miles inland. The adults were specifically reminded that as enemy aliens they would not be allowed to possess a wireless set. It was also indicated that if one was short of funds the government would make an initial payment not exceeding £5 per adult and £2 per child. If necessary a monthly allowance of £10 per adult and £3 per child would be paid, but this would be treated as a loan and subject to repayment when in a position to do so. My parents probably received these allowances, but whether they were ever repaid I do not know.

Although the train journey took about two days I remember little or nothing about it.

8

Tabora

On arrival in Tabora we were taken to the Park Hotel. My grandparents, uncle and aunt were not with us as they had been sent to a different location called Nzega.

It was probably at this hotel that we were put in touch with a local Salvation Army family who would act as our hosts to try to ease our settling in. Brigadier Dare and his wife invited us to tea and I remember admiring their son John's wonderful train set layout. John was a student at the Arusha School and a very good cricket player. He is commemorated on a wooden board displayed in the school dining room which lists him as having climbed Mount Meru.

For some reason we moved house a lot, but our first home in Tabora was on a hill in an area called Rufita. In Tabora water had to be boiled and filtered before it could be drunk. Initially we did the half-hour's walk to the hotel to eat with other refugees, but Mutti quickly decided this was impractical and, as foodstuff was cheap, she could do better cooking at home. Anyway, our cook had to be occupied and would have had to be paid.

Yes, despite the fact that we were refugees and probably destitute except for the government allowance, the expectation was that we would employ servants and arrangements had been made for potential employees to attend the hotel for interview. Most of these would have had references. The usual thing was to have a cook known as the *mpishi* and someone who was referred to in those days as a houseboy, or just 'boy'. There was strict job separation and so one usually also had a *dhobi* to wash the clothes. Wages for staff were low – I have a sum of 20 shillings a month for the houseboy and 30 shillings for the cook in my mind. These shillings were, of course, local currency, though for those who no longer know, a pound sterling in the UK used to be worth 20 shillings. I do not know what the rate of exchange would have been.

On 4th March 1942 Mutti wrote to Omama and told her that the cook had left. Mutti was now preparing the food, and the houseboy, who it turned out was also a cook, then watched over the cooking. The new arrangement was cheaper and in any case, not much different as Mutti said that she had to show the *mpishi* how to do everything anyway. She also employed a *mtoto*, a child who went shopping and was paid 12 shillings.

At some time or other we employed another cook who stayed with us until we finally left Africa. Mutti did not always see eye to eye with him, but they survived each other! He was quite an important person in the local community and people came to him in the afternoon, seemingly for classes of some sort.

In another letter Mutti said that our first house had a downstairs room where the 'boy' could sleep. I seem to recall that with our last home there was rudimentary accommodation nearby which may have been allocated for employee use.

As Tabora was a rail junction it had considerable importance. It was an administrative centre with government departments situated in 'the Boma', as it was known, which was set on a hill. About five roads radiated out from this centre. As well as the railway station there was the hotel, a hospital, a cinema, an English club, an Anglican church and a Roman Catholic mission. There was even a dentist, an elderly German man who was better than nothing, which was the usual situation. The European population was small; I believe about seventy excluding the refugees. The Indian and African populations no doubt were considerably larger.

As racial segregation was in place there was no school we could go to in Tabora. This meant we would have to go to boarding school, so much of this chapter relates to my life during the holidays. I will describe my school experiences later.

Being in Africa meant we were wary of snakes and scorpions. We were told that we should never pick up a stone without moving it first to ensure that there was no scorpion or other unpleasant creature underneath it.

Nor should we slip our feet into shoes or slippers without first upending them. There were also very poisonous snakes about and we were warned especially about the black mamba. One day one was spotted near the house and members of our staff killed it with sticks, approaching it barefooted despite the danger. I can remember, too, that we walked to the cinema in the evening carrying kerosene lamps as the light was supposed to keep lions away. Although I never saw a lion in Tabora, we did hear from time to time that someone had gone missing in the township, presumably eaten by one.

Early on we were introduced to the delicious fruit from the many mango trees which grew there in abundance. It was suggested that a good place to eat the fruit was in a bath!

Because malaria was rampant we were advised to take quinine, and did do so for a time. Houses were also protected by netting over windows and doors, and in addition each bed had its own mosquito net. None of this would have helped if a mosquito had already entered the protected zone, so at dusk the house was sprayed with a hand-operated spray gun using Flit, a pyrethrum-based insecticide which had a potent smell.

My father had many episodes of malaria, though fortunately never the serious form known as blackwater fever. Once when Dad felt very poorly, the doctor came.

He stood in the doorway and, no doubt having listened to the symptoms, said, "Sounds like malaria." My dad was not impressed, but I suspect the doctor was right in his diagnosis.

If I had malaria at all it was only once, but I did have two experiences with the hospital in Tabora. On one occasion when I tried to jump over a culvert I cut my hand very badly, embedding wood splinters and other material in the wound. I had to go to the hospital on a regular basis to have it dressed and the bits of wood removed as they welled up with the pus. When it eventually healed my left little finger was bent and I could not flex the middle and end joints. To make a fist and avoid the finger sticking out I used to tuck it under my ring finger to fold it over. An Italian prisoner of war who may have been a physiotherapist attempted to straighten it out by strapping it tight against a board each evening. It did reduce the flexion deformity but did nothing for the lack of movement; nor could it have done as the tendon must have been cut. The main disadvantage as far as I was concerned was that I could not learn to play the guitar as I could not exert adequate pressure with that finger on the stops – at least that is my excuse.

I also encountered jiggers. These are little creatures which embed themselves in the toe pads, then lay eggs and carry these in a sack. They do not hurt but they itch and have to be removed carefully so as to not to rupture the egg sack. The procedure was to use a needle and open the outer layer of the skin and then lift the jigger out, often leaving sizeable holes in the toe pads which over time would close over. In Tabora Hospital it was one of the African ladies who was deputed to perform this task. I had several jiggers and it did not hurt to get them out, but when it was all over and I saw the cavities I fainted!

Quite early in our stay at Tabora we went to the Roman Catholic mission where some kittens were being disposed of. We picked a beautiful grey-and-white male but the nuns wanted to keep it, so we chose a female kitten instead and called her Mausi. Shortly afterward the nuns had a change of heart and let us have our first choice as well. We were told that they were half-wildcat, but you would not have known it from the male, whom we named Peter. He was a very timid and gentle cat with us who never scratched or showed his claws, but he could deal with mice. On one occasion there were a lot of field mice about and the cats literally had a field day. Mausi went to catch them and Peter finished them off. I suppose Mutti was none too pleased with all the dead bodies about the house.

Peter grew into a beautiful cat with a ruff like a mane around his head. One day he just disappeared, returning a month later. He had gone off into the bush and fended for himself, and presumably came back for a rest. He disappeared again and stayed away for a year or so this time. He finally left, never to return.[19]

Another pet was a very small tortoise. Its method of going down steps was by falling over the edge. If it happened to land on its back it had to lie there till it was found, picked up and turned over.

Sometime in 1942 about three thousand Italian civilian prisoners of war arrived at Tabora and were accommodated in a large purpose-built camp. There was also a camp in Kigoma.

From a work point of view the arrival of the Italian prisoners was useful as jobs were difficult to obtain. My dad had made an unsuccessful attempt to relocate to Kenya to run a sweet factory. Fortunately, however, on 13th August 1942 he was appointed as camp assistant with the rank of assistant

---

19 Lisa's memory with regard to what happened to this cat differs from mine.

inspector of police, despite the enemy alien status! I think his first posting was to Kigoma some two hundred miles further inland, but at some point he was relocated to Tabora where we remained till we left Africa. His initial salary, slightly less than the government allowance mentioned earlier, was £300 per annum with no leave or passage privileges attached. My dad had had a classical education so knew Latin well, and this enabled him to become fluent in Italian relatively easily.

To help him do his job he was provided with a bicycle. He learned to ride but did not seem very confident with his new means of transport. I was allowed to use the bike but because the saddle was too high for me I put my leg through the crossbar to ride it. For a time we were living in a house opposite a building used by the Public Works Department (PWD) which had an S-shaped entry drive. My ambition was to ride down the main road and then take the PWD corner at speed, but I always seemed to apply the brakes and slow down. The day or so before we were to return to school I decided to really master it. I got to the corner, entered it at speed and fell off, slithering across the road which had a sand-and-stone surface. Fortunately I did not suffer any serious injury, but had grazes all over. Not daring to tell my parents, I crept back into the house and washed, presumably thinking they would be angry with me for taking a risk just before setting off to school.

The Italians were gifted artistically and musically and made various items out of wood and ivory, some of which I still have. A small theatre was built in the camp and I saw my first opera there, but annoyingly I cannot recall what it was.

During school holidays one of the prisoners was given permission to come to our house and teach Lisa and me to play a mandolin, possibly made by the Italians in the camp. The mandolin is a lovely instrument and the first time we heard it we were astonished by the sound that could be generated. We were taught the sol-fa notation and only learned the treble clef as we had no occasion to use the bass. A lot of time was spent playing scales and learning to do the tremolo with the plectrum. We learned to play some Neapolitan love songs and a few other pieces such as Schubert and Gounod's *Ave Maria*. As we only played during holiday time, progress was limited.

Tabora boasted an English club, which we did not belong to. It had its own tennis courts but as non-members we would not have been able to use them. Whatever the reasons, two courts were constructed for the refugee families and we learned to play tennis there. Overall this may have turned out to be a good thing as it increased capacity and so made it easier to get a game. The only time I can remember playing at the English club courts was when there was a tennis competition and I was partnered with a lady for the mixed doubles. I was not impressed with her skills. I can still remember trying to play at the net to take as many shots as possible, but it was to no avail and we lost.

At some point two of the Italian prisoners were allowed out to give tennis lessons and training. In the afternoons the adults also played, and we were spoilt as we had ballboys. We also used to play in the morning when the courts were relatively empty. Towards the end of our stay in Tabora we employed a *mtoto* to act as our ballboy.

My dad never played, but Mutti enjoyed the game. She also managed to have words with quite a few of the ladies who played at the tennis courts. Whatever the causes of the arguments, my dad did not like it as he had to work with the husbands. Ironically, I have seen a letter from Mutti in which she comments about the quarrels which were taking place between others and says that it is sad that people cannot be a little more reasonable!

Our tennis courts were partly fenced by straw fencing. During one of our holidays I got hold of some matches and started playing with them, finding that if I lit the straw it burnt very nicely and I could put it out before it got a hold. One time I was not quick enough and lost control of the flames. Fortunately one of the Italian trainers pulled the fencing down and prevented them from spreading further. I was sent home very frightened. Nothing more came of it, but I learned not to play with matches.

Most of our social contact would have been with other refugee families but Mutti did get to know some non-refugee expatriates and we sometimes went to tea with the district commissioner's wife. My recollection is that this was a genteel affair and I would be surprised if we did not have cucumber sandwiches.

There was one refugee family who seemed to us to think themselves a cut above the others. We visited them occasionally as they had children. We must have had a problem with them as I remember I used to lie awake in bed daydreaming about bombing raids, which were in the news at the time, and of having fleets of paper planes which carried out raids over their house. Not perhaps a very kind daydream, but I suppose if they were paper aeroplanes they would also have been paper bombs!

Food, as always, was important to me. During the holidays the *mpishi* used to make a large rice pudding which I enjoyed after our evening meal. I never tired of it, and still enjoy rice puddings. Sometimes too, when resting on my bed during the usual afternoon siesta I used to enjoy lovely bread which my dad had brought back from the camp.

In 1943 Mutti started making sweets at home, including a popular cough sweet flavoured with menthol. My most vivid recollection of the sweet-making dates from about three years later when we had our anti-typhoid jabs in anticipation of our repatriation to Cyprus. I said that these would not have any ill effects, so Mutti boiled up a batch of sweets. Unfortunately I was wrong and it was with aching arms that we had to finish the job.

9

Kigoma

At Tabora, the railway line forked. One branch went to Mwanza and the other to Kigoma on the shores of the long, narrow and very deep Lake Tanganyika lying in the rift valley.

The small port of Kigoma is near a large village called Ujiji. It was here that Stanley met Livingstone with the famous remark, "Dr Livingstone, I presume?" Unfortunately I never managed to see Ujiji or the memorial to Livingstone near Tabora. I somehow learned that when he died, his faithful retainers buried his heart near Tabora and then continued to carry his body down to the coast so that it could be returned to England for burial. I hope I have got this right!

I think I must have been at school when my parents moved to Kigoma as I can only remember a school holiday period there. We had been allocated a house a little way from the lake, with an African thatch roof and no electricity. For light we used pressure and oil lamps.

The cats accompanied my parents. My most vivid recollection is of the cook standing near the house and calling out, "*Nyama, nyama*" (which means 'meat, meat' in Swahili). The cats understood this perfectly and they used to come bounding across the fields to be fed.

There was another refugee family in Kigoma and I was a friend of their daughter Elfrieda, known as Elfie. Somehow Elfie and I managed to get a packet of cigarettes, hid behind a shed and smoked them one after the other as fast as we could so that we would not be caught. Although I smoked four and half cigarettes I was not sick; nor were we found out, but that was my one and only sustained attempt at smoking. I did try a puff or two on a few other occasions after that but never saw anything in it, and once I became a Christian I thought it was wrong anyway, which I suppose helped.

At Kigoma I also attempted to fish in the lake, but with our primitive home-made lines I caught nothing. In truth I was relieved, for I dreaded the thought of handling the fish once it was caught on the line. That was the end of my fishing career.

My parents' return to Tabora must have occurred while we were at school, as again I have no memory of the move.

10

Arusha

Our schooling recommenced in the spring of 1942 at the European co-educational Anglican mission school in Arusha. The town was located at the foot of the 4,300-metre-high Mount Meru. Mount Kilimanjaro, the highest peak in Africa, was about fifty miles away, so just too far to be visible.

Kilimanjaro's main peak, Kibo, is rounded and white as it is permanently covered with snow. Its lower peak, Mawenzi, looks blue-black in contrast. Legend has it that Mawenzi was the wife of Kibo, and had been beaten by him.

Arusha had much to commend it. It was at an elevated location and so climatically was much more benign. There was a small river flowing through it, and our school was built close to one of its banks. Water was clean and so could be drunk from the tap. There was at least one tarmac road and a small hospital, though as far as I remember, no resident dentist. Close to the school was an army camp, and we could sometimes see convoys of military trucks driving in.

The New Arusha Hotel claimed to be located at the centre of Africa. We were occasionally taken there for a meal and I seem to remember that it had a sunken dining room where you could eat your way through the menu from top to bottom, and that they served curries accompanied by a multitude of side dishes. The local Anglican church was within easy walking distance from our school.

11

Travel To and From Arusha School

As it usually took us about two days to travel to school, we had to be boarders. Some children lived even further afield and their journey took considerably longer, for there was no air transport in those days that I am aware of.

I did not dislike the travelling; it was just leaving Mutti that I could not bear. As a result, most school holidays were interspersed with me pleading with her not to send me back. Getting on the train at Tabora was terrible, but I was also a realist. Once the train pulled out of the station I settled straight away and never gave it another thought till the next time. It must have been awful for Mutti, who of course did not see the transformation on the train.

Mutti accompanied us to school on one occasion, perhaps hoping for a bit of a holiday. She was given a guest room in the girls' building. Unfortunately I made her life a misery during her stay as I wanted to be with her all the time and cried and pleaded with her to take me home. As boys were not allowed into the girls' building I went round the outside very early before the rising bell and threw stones at the window to wake her up and get her to come down to me. In the end I suppose she could not stand it and decided to leave. I took a tearful farewell in the headmaster's study, cried for a few minutes after she left and then returned to my class and that was it!

The steam-train journeys were comfortable. Passengers were allocated to either two-berth or four-berth compartments. During the daytime the upper berths were flush against the walls to form comfortable backrests; then at night they were made into equally comfortable beds. The dining car had several sittings for meals which we really enjoyed.

We could stick our heads out of the compartment windows as it was a single-line track, but soot from the engine was a menace and so we did not spend too much time doing this. The wind was, however, refreshing in the heat.

At stops vendors were trying to sell their wares, and at times we did buy little things that as children we could afford. It was at Kilimatinde that I bought a little black crocodile which we still display at home.

I remember that I saw children with protruding tummies and I presumably thought that they were well fed. Probably though, they were suffering from the protein-deficiency disease kwashiorkor, which occurs when one's food contains enough carbohydrates but not enough proteins.

Sitting on the train to or from Dodoma for several hours, however comfortable, does get boring, so we passed the time by playing various games and eating. At times the games were a bit boisterous. Once one of the girls was throwing my sister's overcoat about and it flew straight out of the open window! The coat had come with us from Vienna so I was extremely angry and hit the girl on the nose and made it bleed. I imagine the supervising adult intervened.

Dodoma was important for us as it was the intersection for the road and rail part of our journey, and we quite often spent a night in the hotel there. The town of Dodoma has grown in importance and is now officially the capital of Tanzania. At that time it was the seat of the Anglican Bishop of Central Tanganyika, and there was a large mission station at Mvumi nearby which I visited once.

We were of course accompanied by adults, but we quickly developed a lot of self-confidence and considered ourselves seasoned and experienced travellers. Nevertheless we were still children, and it showed at times. One evening, wandering about across the railway lines, we came to a train turntable. In it there were a lot of scorpions and we decided that we should throw stones at them. Someone saw us and sent us packing. I suppose we could have damaged or jammed the machinery, apart from hurting the scorpions.

The train journey was only about half the distance and the remaining 275 miles were by road. Except for a few miles near Arusha, none of the road was tarmacked. During the dry season the road was easily passable, if a bit rough, but when it rained it could become a quagmire. One journey stands out when we got stuck several times and had to get out and push the vehicles to get them going.

We travelled on the back of lorries; no comfortable coaches in those days! How many vehicles depended on how many children were travelling, and this did seem to vary. At one time it used to be three with one lorry carrying the luggage and just a few children. It was great if we could get on this one as we could arrange the cases to make a sort of couch and feel the wind on our faces. The other lorries had wooden seats along the sides. I can remember that it was cold when we got up early in Arusha to start our journey home, and the lorry's tarpaulin roofing, supported on a central wooden beam, was left in place. I hated this as the canvas tended to hit you on the head. It also restricted sight and air. The canvas was usually removed once it became warmer.

For whatever reason I remember more of my return journeys from Arusha. The first one hundred miles consisted of large tracts of grassland or savannas similar to those found in the Serengeti. There were huge populations of wildebeest, zebras and gazelles, and no doubt carnivorous animals too but I never saw any on this part of the journey. We then rested and shopped at a small place called Babati.

The next seventy-five miles or so was hilly, and called Pina Heights. It was here that we passed through part of the rift valley, a huge geological fault stretching for thousands of miles. Lake Tanganyika lies in one of its branches, but this is hundreds of miles from the road between Arusha and Dodoma. In places the walls of the rift valley could be clearly seen.

Most of us were reasonable travellers but one poor girl called Annalise used to be terribly carsick. There was not much space and on at least one occasion she lay on the floor of the lorry at our feet. I had been a good traveller until the time I bought a tin of sweetened condensed milk at Babati. I punched two holes in it and as we trundled along towards and across the Pina Heights I drank it all. It was a bad mistake as I felt very sick for the whole time that we traversed the mountain section. I never did this again, but always thereafter felt sick when we crossed the Pina Heights towards Dodoma. However, I still like sweetened condensed milk!

The final hundred miles to Dodoma was mainly through shrub and bushland. There were fewer animals here, but on one occasion our vehicle suddenly stopped, and there on the road behind us was a lioness, or perhaps a lion. For a few moments we looked at each other and then the animal wandered off into the bush and we drove on.

Because we traversed an area where the tsetse fly was endemic, precautions were taken to avoid it spreading to other parts of the country. This fly spreads yellow fever, which is a serious illness. At the start of the infected zone and at its exit, there were sheds. The lorry was driven in, the doors closed and the lorry and its occupants were sprayed with insecticide!

On the whole, we used to enjoy the journeys and sang songs to pass the time of day. *She'll Be Coming 'Round the Mountain* and *It's a Long Way to Tipperary* spring to mind.

12

Arusha School

Until I was about ten I had never attended any school for longer than one year, sometimes with long gaps in my education. I was at Arusha from 1942 to 1946. I enjoyed my time there and believe it turned out to be pivotal in my life.

The school was modelled on an English public school and most of the students were boarders. The main building formed two quadrangles, divided by the dining room. The boys' dormitories were situated in this building, while the girls were housed separately. There was one playing field, a tennis court, and a swimming pool which was very popular. At one end of the playing field was a very large avocado tree suitable for climbing, but as I did not like the fruit at that time, nor was I good at climbing, I did not get much benefit from it. Beneath the tree lived a giant tortoise which was strong enough to carry a child. Not an exciting ride as it was so slow!

We were free to wander within the school grounds which were reasonably extensive, but the river which flowed alongside one boundary and the town were out of bounds. The river was not very large but once we had about five inches of rain in one night and it became a raging torrent, which was exciting to see. There were also occasional earthquakes but we never suffered damage or injury.

During the five years or so that I was at the school we had five headmasters. Rev. Wynn Jones moved on to become a bishop, as, I think, did Rev. Langford Smith. Between these, Major Lace held the reins. He had the reputation of only smiling once a year on speech day, and then only slightly. Rev. Phillips had a fierce temper and I was a bit wary of him. The acting head when we left was Mr Doran.

The children were divided into two houses, imaginatively called North and South, and of course there was intense rivalry between them. I was in North. The uniform included a blue blazer with an embroidered badge sporting the school motto, which was *Seeking the Highest*. I longed to have one but did not get it because of the war. We wore khaki shorts and the girls khaki gymslips.

The only English-speaking school Lisa and I had been to prior to this was the American Academy in Larnaca when we were six years old. Mutti did try to educate us at home and sought to ensure that we could speak English, but I do not know how fluent we were when we first got to our new school.

I have found a letter in English which I think I wrote before we went to Arusha. It was in an envelope with a letter from Mutti dated 4th March 1942.

Liebe Omama [Dear Grandma],
Hwo [sic; how] are you! My mother said that I shall write you.
I am learning foot-ball. And Mr Duldner comes to us.
I am going to every foot-ball match and every Hokey- match Lisa is lli [sic; ill].
Kindest regards to you and your family.
Your Stefan Popper.

The misspellings are quite interesting as I have at times wondered if I was a little dyslexic.

Going to this school was the first time that I had been away from Mutti. I was lucky of course because Lisa was also at the school, but I may have been a bit lonely because I can remember how happy I was when I awoke one morning to learn that a new boy had come who turned out to be my friend Peter Hoffer.

In the dormitories, children were grouped more or less according to age. By our beds we had a chair with a hinged seat, and a locker for immediate necessities in the compartment beneath the seat. The rest of our clothing was stored in a linen room ruled by Matron and shared by some bats! Near the dorms was a communal washroom with several wash basins and toilets, and so washing and going to the toilets often became quite a social affair.

There were dorm and school prefects who had positions of authority and importance within the school structure. Even so, there was some bullying. Once two lads decided to pick on me. One was stronger than me, but the other weaker. I decided to defend myself by grabbing the weaker boy, wrestling him to the ground and then banging his head on the concrete floor every time the other one hit me. His tears soon caused the other lad to stop, and once the incident was over I do not recall any bad blood between us.

The first end-of-term report I can find is for the second term of 1942. Bearing in mind that we did not get to Tabora till late December 1941, we probably began school in late April or early May 1942, which may well coincide with the beginning of that term.

The rising bell was at 6.30am. Sometimes we had physical activities before breakfast. Putting on our shorts in the cold immediately on waking was not popular, so we were glad when these activities came to an end. At another time we were expected to run, or in my case more usually walk, to the school boundary where a senior girl was responsible for ticking us off a register.

After breakfast there were domestic duties including bed-making and getting ready for an inspection. We then went to assembly, which included hymn-singing, prayers and usually a spiritual talk. This was also an opportunity for mail distribution, notices, and the public awarding of stars (commendations) and stripes (rebukes) which featured in the inter-house competition. I cannot remember getting many stars, but then nor did I get many stripes.

Then lessons till lunchtime, interrupted by a short break where we were given something to eat, usually bananas, guavas or granadillas[20]. The rest of the break was spent in the quads wrestling, flying paper aeroplanes or just doing our own thing.

After the siesta, where the dorm prefects ensured we lay down, there was afternoon school until about 4pm; then a further break with fruit. Once a boy complained that he was not getting enough. He was sat down to a great pile of bananas and allowed to eat as much as he wished. When he had finished he was expelled, though hopefully not for good! In the

20 Passion fruit.

afternoon we could also get goodies from our tuck shop, so we were certainly not starved.

Organised games followed: football, cricket or hockey depending on the term. I hated cricket as I could neither field, bat nor bowl and was scared of the fast bowlers. My highest score was four runs. I was not good at football either, but did enjoy hockey, being moderately good at it.

I enjoyed swimming, particularly underwater. I once swam a mile in a supervised event, but sadly have to admit that I cheated as I put my feet down in the shallow end. I was not spotted, so was given credit for this achievement.

Athletics also featured but I was hopeless at this too, though I had to join in. In the fiercely contested inter-house games I was only ever selected for the tug of war as I was always on the heavy side.

For variety we went on cross-country runs and paperchases, which again I disliked. It did not help that I was a bit scared of the Masai. In those days they still walked about in long cloaks carrying their spears and covered with fat or something which gave off a pungent odour. One day a Masai came onto the playing field and I bought some brown sugar from him, for which I was caned. Another time a few of us met a group who I think were about to initiate some of their young men. They ran over to us and started pointing, but we decided to run and were relieved when they did not follow.

Sometimes we ran along the railway lines. These crossed deep ravines and we had to step from sleeper to sleeper to get across. We could see the ravine through the gaps, and sometimes I was too petrified to move. Finally I would crawl across on all fours. Because I was so slow I probably worried that a train would come, but presumably the teachers knew it was safe to let us onto the line.

After games we got ready for supper, following which there might be homework, but also some free time. The day finished with the evening assembly, again with hymn-singing, prayers and usually a talk. Bedtime depended on age, but the latest was 8.30pm. I can remember lying in bed and hearing the radio in the dining room play *Hearts of Oak*, which was the signature tune for the BBC 9pm news. And so to sleep.

There was no formal teaching at the weekend. Saturday morning was spent getting ready for the major inspection of the week. This involved making our beds most carefully and laying out the contents of our lockers. We also sat in the sun polishing our shoes and blancoing (i.e. whitening) our plimsolls, which could take quite a time.

After siesta, the afternoon was free. On Saturday the games cupboard was opened and we were given access to sports equipment. We also played made-up games including Cops and Robbers. Sometimes we put on an impromptu concert in which my contribution was usually telling a joke. At other times we might have a lantern slide show. The light for the slide projector had to be produced on site. A chemical mixed with water produced a gas, which had a disagreeable smell before being ignited but then gave a very bright light.

There were a number of Jewish refugee families in Arusha who sometimes invited us out for tea, and Saturday afternoon was a convenient time for this. Of course we had to get permission to leave school grounds.

When we first got to school the only drink at meals apart from water was tea, which I hated. One day I went to a birthday party at the New Arusha Hotel and was offered coffee. I drank perhaps six to eight cups, ignoring even the cakes in favour of coffee. That night I wandered round the quad for some time, fortunately undetected, before I could get to sleep.

Sunday was a day of rest. Morning service at Christ Church was compulsory, though I think Roman Catholic children were exempt. We dressed up in our Sunday best, were inspected to see that the turnout was okay, and marched smartly in a military fashion to church. I found the service long and boring but I did usually listen to the blessing on the principle that a blessing could not do me any harm!

One Sunday another boy and I decided to skip church – very ironic in the light of what happened later. Somehow we slipped out of the line of marching children and hid. We enjoyed our spare time and the excitement and apprehension which no doubt went with it.

We managed to get away with it for a while, but were eventually caught and penalised. We were not allowed to talk during mealtimes and also had to learn the Ten Commandments off by heart. I had only learned a bit when the teacher came to ask how I was getting on. My reply, to the effect that I was getting there, satisfied him, so I could talk at mealtimes again. My companion replied rather differently, implying that he had not learned them yet, and as a result he was still banned from talking. I am afraid after that I did not apply myself any further to the task of memorising the commandments.

On the whole, we did not like Sunday afternoons as activities were restricted. We read or played our own games. Sometimes we just sat on the playing field, talking and sucking grass stalks in a desultory sort of manner. Sometimes Mr Chittleborough, who was an extremely keen and devout Christian, came and sat with a group and tried to evangelise us. Most of the teachers had Christian convictions, and as this was a mission school there was a very strong emphasis on Christian teaching. Not all parents approved of this.

Grass was not the only free outdoor meal available. There were the avocados, and for those who liked them flying ants could be caught and grilled on the tilley lamps in the evenings. This was not a taste I acquired.

On at least two occasions enormous swarms of locusts like large dark clouds passed over Arusha. They did not settle in any numbers, but of those that did I now wonder (though I cannot really remember) whether, if one can grill flying ants, some may have been turned into a feast and so never reached their final destination.

As one would expect, the school had a sick bay staffed by a nurse. There was a time when more or less the whole school got conjunctivitis and had to have their eyes irrigated with saline for a few days. I enjoyed being allowed to help with the treatment.

At times we were required to take quinine. As it was to prevent malaria I wonder why we did not take it all the time, but on the other hand perhaps that was a good thing as quinine can be ototoxic. For a while only liquid quinine was available, and taking that is an art form as it is so bitter. I learned to pour it to the back of my mouth, and that worked well.

Over the years there were outbreaks of mumps, measles, whooping cough and chickenpox, and so many children were ill at once that some of the dormitories were turned into wards. My timing for mumps was bad as I did not develop symptoms until I had returned home for a holiday. Mutti felt sorry for me but could not help laughing because I looked so funny with my swollen parotid glands.

My only visit to the local hospital in Arusha was for a tooth extraction when a dentist and anaesthetist were present. Chloroform was used and simply dripped onto a mask on my face. Luckily I liked the smell so it was no great problem. However, post extraction I had a lot of pain in the nights which only stopped when the term ended after a few days and I returned home.

Children who lived too far away had to stay at school for half-term. During one of these breaks we had been taken swimming in a nearby lake on a coffee plantation, and I stepped on some stiff grass and punctured my foot. Coming up soon was a climb to the first hut on Mount Meru, which was a day's walk there and back. Although I was not a great walker, usually ending up at the tail end, I did not want to be left out. So I decided to try to dig out the offending piece of grass with a pin or needle which I sterilised with a match. I went on the hike with no problem.

Sometime later Major Lace, the headmaster, was supervising our football. He thought I was not running enough and came up behind me, grabbed me by the scruff of the neck and ran me along the field, a habit of his when he felt a child was not putting enough into the game. Afterwards a large painful swelling came up on the ball of my foot. Rightly or wrongly, I have always blamed this excessive activity. As there were no antibiotics available in those days, the treatment was to soak the foot in hot water in which potassium permanganate crystals had been dissolved. I assume it was also dressed with something to draw the pus out.

Unfortunately the term ended before my foot had fully cleared up and I had to stay at school for a few extra days, thus missing the return trip home. I was lucky as I was invited to stay with a new scholar, a Polish boy called Zygmund who lived only about fifty miles away in Moshi at the foot of Mount Kilimanjaro.

Two things made my stay memorable. I learned to play draughts. My friend's aunt was a good player and I nagged her to play for hours with me till I learned her technique. Also, the family ran a café-restaurant and provided chess sets for their guests. One day I overheard a couple discussing in Greek whether they should steal one of the sets. Of course they did not realise that I could understand them. Feeling quite pleased with myself, I just got up and carried the set away.

I am convinced that academically the standards at the school were high and I owe a lot to the thorough and extensive education I received.

When we arrived Lisa and I started off in Standard III. At the end of the year Lisa was promoted to Standard IV, but despite the fact that I did better than an older boy in the year I was left behind and he was promoted. Although I was upset, it turned out to be for the best as at the end of the next year I was awarded the third-place prize. It was the only academic achievement that I got at that school.

I tended to do well in those subjects that I liked. Among these were arithmetic, geography, history, scripture and elementary science, especially biology, driving the teacher crazy at times with my questions and interjections.

English literature included Shakespeare, and I remember doing *A Midsummer Night's Dream* and *The Tempest*. Composition was never a strong point with me; nor was the quality of my writing and spelling.

I was abysmal at drawing and painting, not helped because I was colour-blind. Once I was very upset when I only scored 2%, having carefully drawn and coloured the furniture of a room. When I complained it turned out that I had painted it crimson, mistaking that colour in the paintbox for brown. Today my work might be deemed creative! The only time when I got a decent mark was when the teacher read an extract from *The Snow Goose* by Paul Gallico and told us to draw a picture based on it. I was fascinated by the story about the Dunkirk evacuation and, with a little help from the teacher, did a reasonable job.

Singing was another failure. My first shattering experience was in my first year when I tried to join the choir. The teacher suddenly stopped us singing, pointed at me and told me to get out. My inability to sing was confirmed, for when my voice was breaking it was suggested that I leave the classroom and try to learn to play an instrument instead. I chose the flute, but my progress was limited to just managing to get a sound out and perhaps a scale or two.

Practical subjects included carpentry. Here I was unable even to plane six sides of a piece of wood to the required standard, and so was reduced to sharpening plane blades for more gifted boys.

At one point boxing became the in thing. My dad also seems to have thought this a useful skill, and during some of the holidays an Italian came to give me lessons and training. It did not help. I was a miserable failure and during a competition I spent the entire time retreating or running away so as not to get hurt.

After the war ended, photographic supplies must again have become available because as an extracurricular activity Mr Chittleborough taught some of us how to develop film and print pictures. We did not have an enlarger so scope was limited, but I enjoyed it and later in life made use of the teaching I had received.

We could join the Scouts or the Guides if we wished. For a term or so we learned fencing using wooden sticks instead of swords. I enjoyed this, but was not so inspired by another activity which involved making mud bricks!

In the autumn of 1945 an inter-school competition was arranged under the auspices of the Indian Youth League which included an elocution contest. This was not easy as it involved picking a subject out of a hat and addressing an audience in the local cinema on it for two minutes. I entered for this and was advised to try to prepare an opening sentence which would fit any subject as this would give me time to think about what to say next. I drew farming, a subject I knew next to nothing about. To my surprise, when we attended the prize-giving I was given a certificate. It was either second or third prize as the certificate mentions both! This was the second and final prize I ever won whilst at the school.

Winning gave me confidence in public speaking. I became the chosen student speaker if one was needed at school, and this probably laid the foundation for much of my public speaking in later life.

Lisa did rather better academically than me and always remained a year ahead of me. By 1946 we were reaching the top of the school. Secondary education was available in Kenya but not in Tanganyika. Lisa and I had expected to take the entrance examination, but at the last moment we were told that as enemy aliens we would not be allowed to go to the schools in Kenya. Our school arranged for us to sit the papers anyway and the head confirmed that on their marking we both would have been successful.

Having been marched into the dining room by the prefects, at mealtimes we sat at our allocated places at long wooden tables which were under the charge of a teacher, except in the evening when the prefects presided. Grace was said before and after each meal.

Initially water was the only alternative to tea, but later on we did get served coffee and sometimes even cocoa. I only started drinking tea after I became a prefect, and then only in the evening. Seated at the head of one of the junior tables, I was served tea in a teapot with a sugar bowl and separate milk so that I could make it to my taste. It made me feel important to be treated like the staff!

It was the rule that we had to finish everything on our plates. One poor boy who hated nearly all the puddings sometimes sat alone in the dining room, trying to finish up his meal. The rule led to a mass rebellion when instead of the popular mashed papaya we were served with mashed pumpkin, which looked the same but tasted awful. Hardly anyone ate it and in the end the children won.

For a while I sat at a table supervised by a music teacher who was not too particular about enforcing the rule. I enjoyed eating up unwanted portions of eggs and bacon which happened to be served at that time. It should not have happened, but I approved.

There must also have been shortages. At one time we were allocated two slices of bread with our breakfast and evening meals, only one of which was spread with butter or margarine.

Mealtimes were pleasurable as we could chat or tell each other stories. If it got too noisy, order was imposed. As we became more senior we progressed up the room towards the head table. Sitting at this was considered a real privilege.

The staff had their evening meal in the staffroom. To my eyes this meal was superior, but having said this I think our food was good and we grew and thrived on it.

On the whole I got on well with the teachers, though there was one I was rather scared of as he had a short temper.

I was very fond of Sister Cloudsdale, a Church Army sister who was matron for a time. Two incidents I remember with some shame as I think of her. At one time tinned lobster was in plentiful supply and also very cheap, so I could buy it with my pocket money. Sister Cloudsdale hated it, and for a prank I hid some loose lobster under her pillow. She must have been a very forgiving person as I do not remember any repercussions.

Then on her birthday I promised her that I would bring hot water for her bath from the children's bathroom, from where it had to be carried in large jerrycans. I forgot to do so and was very sorry that I had let her down. Even now, after so many years, I still regret this.

Corporal punishment was the headmaster's prerogative and we were caned on our backsides through our clothes. The maximum number of strokes was six. The punishment was a very effective deterrent and only used rarely.

Major Lace, however, although no doubt a good teacher, was a rather austere man in my eyes and sometimes thought up unusual punishments.

Lisa told me that on one occasion he sent a child out of the class and said, "Go and eat grass." He looked out after a while and was astonished to see the boy actually doing so. Sucking grass, as I have remarked earlier, was after all quite an enjoyable pastime.

When I became a prefect I looked after one of the dormitories for the younger boys and was allowed to mete out limited punishment if they did not behave. I used to extend the siesta time on Saturday afternoon so that they could not go out to play. However, my bark was worse than my bite because I quite often let them off some of the punishment at the end. I also used to make a weekly bathing rota for my dorm. I took this very seriously and spent a lot of time trying to make the rota fair so that the good slots were shared around.

As is usual in a co-educational school, there was a lot of teasing about boyfriends and girlfriends. When my friend Ulli joined the school I decided that the best form of defence was attack and told her to tell everyone that she was my girlfriend. It seemed to have worked as I do not recall any teasing, but neither do I remember spending very much time with her either.

My first real love was a slightly older Greek girl called Eva Fieros. I worshipped her from afar, just trying to meet her casually during break times or when she was the checker at the end of our morning runs. She left the school before I did and went to Limuru Girls' School in Kenya. We did correspond for some years after she left, and the letters consist mainly but not exclusively of Bible studies. Eventually Eva married Michael Woods and my last letter to her was written in the early '50s, after which we lost touch for many years.

Life, however, has odd ways of turning out. When we had returned to Cyprus after the war, my dentist happened to mention that relatives from Africa were visiting. My heart leapt and I asked if their name was Fieros. Indeed it was, but Eva was by then already married and only her mother and sister had come. It was in the 1990s that by chance at a funeral I met a former Arusha School student who gave me Eva's address in London. I was thrilled, and have since occasionally met both her and her husband.

13

Conversion to Christianity

Religious instruction played a major part in school life, but on the whole passed us by. The boys swore like troopers, fought and did the usual naughty things. I do not know about the girls, but suppose it was not that different. As shown by my truancy from church, I was if anything less keen than others, but I did occasionally when I was in bed at night think about what we had been taught about Heaven, Hell and that Jesus could be our Saviour. However, I did nothing about it.

Things changed dramatically, however, at the beginning of the first term of 1945 when I went down with a bad case of chickenpox. I was doused with calamine lotion to ease the itching of my countless spots.

I was told that it would take three weeks before I would be better and let out of quarantine, but also that I would have to wait till all the spots had disappeared. Three weeks came and went. Over the days I became anxious that God would not let me get better and so I was at risk of going to Hell as I had not taken notice of the school's teaching about the need to receive Jesus as Saviour. I decided that I would try to give up one sin per day, thinking that it would not take long to become perfect and hoping that God would then be pleased with me. However, I knew in my heart that this was not the way to be 'born again' as a Christian and as I continued to have spots, one night while lying in bed I decided to accept the Lord Jesus into my heart as Saviour. I may have been wrong about the reason for not getting better, but I believe that God used this opportunity to bring me into a relationship with Himself. Becoming a

Christian is the most important thing that has ever happened to me, and changed my life.

Shortly after this, I returned to normal schooling. As I feared that I would be teased by the other children, I initially kept quiet about my decision. One evening after prayers I confided in a boy who I thought might be sympathetic. He assured me of secrecy, but it did not take long before the whole school seemed to know. The time had come to choose whether I would stick with my decision, and I did.

A lot of things changed for me over the next months. I stopped swearing completely. On the other hand, while I was trying to read during siesta time swear words spontaneously appeared on the page. I felt that this was an attack of the Devil, and on advice I stopped reading for a while. When this seemed to work I restarted with a couple of books about missionary work. Hudson Taylor's work in China was very heavy going, but the life of C. T. Stubbs was much more interesting. I had the little Red Letter New Testament which I had been given in Palestine, and I started to read that too.

Later, I asked Mr Chittleborough how many times he had read the Bible through, and he said he thought about three times. Being ambitious I wanted to catch up and so decided to read two chapters of the Old Testament and one of the New each day, but each chapter three times over. I was also very particular about the way I read, trying to look at each word as I took the Bible to be the word of God. So my siesta was a very busy time.

Now, instead of avoiding church, I would have liked to go to evensong as well if I had been allowed. I discovered a room in the school that had been set aside as a chapel, and started to go there for prayer before the evening assembly. I used to make sure that the kneelers were all properly aligned; in fact I was as obsessive about this as I was about my Bible-reading. After I had gone to bed I said my evening prayers kneeling up in bed. As the beds were encased in mosquito nets it was not practical to kneel outside, and besides, it was warmer under the blankets.

Because of my interest I was allowed to go to some Bible studies held by some of the teachers. Eva used to go to these as well, which was a bonus as far as I was concerned. These studies were the model for our later correspondence.

At one time I was involved with a Sunday school which we held at the school after church. For a time we had a very good response to this.

Because of the Christian atmosphere at school, and also the ordered way of life there, I found it easier there than I did at home. Not that my parents were difficult or tried to stop me, but there was less Christian input.

After a while I decided that I wanted to get baptised. I must have written home for permission as I have a letter about this in German from my dad, dated 18th February 1946. He was concerned that I was under the influence of Mr Chittleborough and said he would prefer me to be baptised after I had left school to make sure it was my decision. It was an entirely legitimate point. I have to say I was very fortunate with my parents as they did not try to dissuade me or put obstacles in my way.

I replied[21] at length. I am very glad that Mutti kept this letter safe, which is why I still have it. There had obviously been a wide-ranging conversation with Mr Chittleborough, which I tried to summarise for my dad and then wrote, *maybe it does not sound convincing on paper but it really is. You don't know I don't think how you feel when Jesus talks to you because there is one half of you tells you one thing and other half the other, and it is quite difficult not to go onto the devils side.*

I then talked about translating his letter, and continued, *Please will you send me ten shillings and if you want a few extra ones as well...* Later in the letter I came back to this, and it turns out that I needed the money to pay for a concordance Bible which I had bought with my dad's permission.

There then follows a long section in which I tell my dad that most of the school was going to the cinema. I tell him I am not going and explain, *it is not a punishment, but I don't think it is right for me to go this time may be it will not be right for me to go at all anymore, but that does not matter because Jesus will give me something much better and I must grow in grace and in faith which means sometimes to give things up.* Later on I admit, *Really I want to go very much but that was me and the devil and not Jesus and I have to do what Jesus wants and not what I want. This might also give me a chance of preaching as a lot of people might start teasing me and if I am strong enough I should be able to preach to them. I would be so happy if you Mother and Lisa became Christians and followed Jesus with all your heart as well.*

For whatever reasons, I had concerns about the cinema visit. Looking at all this now there is obviously an element of negativity about this, but it sprang from my desire for a deeper relationship with God.

---

21 The letter is dated 26th February 1945, obviously in error as it was 1946.

I was, however, still only thirteen, and the letter ends, *There is nothing much here. I might be in the first eleven to play against the club on Saturday. We had a tennis tournament and Trixie beat me 8 9 but that doesn't matter either.* There is a postscript: *this was a very long letter &I want translate the letter now because I am too lazy.*[22]

I have perhaps over-quoted from this letter, but it gives a clearer insight into what I thought and how I felt at that time than if I tried to write about it any other way. It also shows that I did not find it easy. I often felt unsure as to whether I had made a true and full commitment, and so at times used to reaffirm my faith as I felt (and still feel) that a relationship with God matters.

In his letter my dad made no mention of the fact that we had actually been baptised in Vienna, but he must at some point have either told me or the school, and instead of being baptised I was confirmed. In those days before being confirmed one had to learn the catechism more or less by heart. This included the Ten Commandments, and so my previous punishment probably came in very useful. Bishop Chambers of the Diocese of Central Tanganyika conducted the confirmation service at Christ Church, Arusha.

---

22   Editors note: Errors in the quoted letter have not been corrected

14

Lisa's Account of Our Early Years

Lisa in 1938 aged 6

When I first started writing, Lisa said she would write up an account too. She did not want to look at what I had written as she felt it would cloud her own memories. She thought it would be a good idea to put the accounts back to back. I did not argue about it but I think I was not that keen – perhaps I feared her account might be better than mine!

Sadly Lisa died in 2006 and she never saw what I had written. As she had never shown anything to me I thought that she had not written anything down, but then I found an account on her computer covering our lives from birth to Arusha.

Some of the incidents she recounts I recognise, others I had forgotten, and still others I do not remember at all. Also in places she remembers facts differently to me. In some cases (but by no means all) where our recollections differ I have added footnotes, but unsurprisingly I prefer my version when we differ.

I have avoided making spelling corrections or other editorial changes except where really necessary, but have tried to complete blanks.

I have wondered where to insert her account and think this may be a good place to do so as her story ends during our stay at Arusha School. I am sorry that she was unable to complete it.

I hope that it will be read.

★★★

A Refugee of Long Ago

I am writing this in the spring of 1999, a time of war and above all of refugees.

Refugees have existed since time immemorial and I too belong to that unhappy band. In 1938, however, one had to have some means to be a refugee, at least if one was a Jew in a Nazi-occupied country: means to buy one's way out of one's native country and then more means to buy one's way into another country. The facts in this saga are taken from old documents but the things that happened are described through the eyes of a very young and very frightened and confused child. However, let me start at the beginning.

My twin brother, Stefan, and I were born in Vienna in May 1932. Stefan has the unusual privilege of having two birth certificates, each showing a different place of arrival in this world; the first being the hospital, the second being our home address. By the time I came along eleven minutes later, only the home address was available.[23]

We lived in the heart of Vienna, just off the Kaerntnerstrasse (Vienna's main shopping street) at Rauhensteingasse 8. The house was called Mozarthof, as Mozart had lived and died there.

---

23 In fact, her original birth certificate shows the hospital address as I have photocopies of this. I expect a reissue shows the home address.

Stefan and Lisa 1933

I do not remember much of the house, except that there were countless stairs to go up and down, as a huge bust of Mozart took up the room on the ground floor normally reserved for a lift. I have found out since that we lived on the fourth floor.

My parents were well off and we lived in a large flat and had a cook, a maid and of course a nanny, whom we called Detta. I remember our room clearly; it was on two levels. On entering one encountered the lower level, where stood our two cots, fairly far apart, plus chests of drawers and cupboards which held our clothes. A small step brought one to the upper level, where our toys were kept and where we played. There was a large window which ran along the entire width of this part, making it very light. I remember spending many happy hours at this window admiring the raindrop patterns and ice flowers which formed during the very cold Austrian winters. Off to the side was a door which brought one straight into the kitchen. I remember very little of the kitchen, except that we had our hair washed there (which I hated because I always got soap in my eyes) and that it was where we cleaned our shoes.

To get to my mother's room meant walking across a corridor, through a large and heavily furnished dining room (which I hated walking through because it was so dark) and then into my mother`s bedroom. We usually went there only to say goodnight.

My father, who was a lawyer, had his offices in the flat and I can remember nothing of them, but I can remember Stefan and myself visiting his room in the mornings and having him tell us stories. He also came and played the gramophone for us in the evenings (we had an old wind-up machine on one of the chests of drawers in our room). But what I enjoyed most was him reading poetry and books to us, a particular favourite of mine being *The Story of Doctor Doolittle*.

Besides the flat, which was rented, our parents owned a small bathing hut with garden in a place called Kritzendorf. We never actually went there (although our parents used to spend weekends there), but it was to play a big role prior to our leaving Vienna.

During the morning we went out to the Stadtpark with our Detta, whom we adored, where we played and ran about, and in the afternoons my mother often took us to our maternal grandparents' restaurant-cum-coffee shop. My grandparents were co-owners, the other partner being my mother's uncle Marcus Klug. This was a very large and forward-looking establishment called the Kaffee Herrenhof located in the Herrengasse, which takes one to the Michaelerplatz where the Hofburg is situated. My grandparents were very innovative and had many splendid dances in the downstairs ballroom, as well as being instrumental in bringing Russian musicians to Vienna for the first time. One of the things I particularly enjoyed on these visits was when my grandmother took me to what I suppose was the larder and gave me a few raisins. However, one of the things I was given which I disliked, and which always gave me a headache, was Vienna's famous whipped cream.

I liked my grandmother and enjoyed being considered old enough to be allowed away from the strict supervision of Detta or Mother.

The Kaffee Herrenhof still exists in vestigial form and serves excellent Viennese food.[24]

---

24   By 2008 this was no more.

In the winter my mother also took us skating, which I loved. When walking home in the dark, if we had been very good, we were bought some hot chestnuts from a street vendor and a few of these held in a muff did wonders for defrosting little fingers.

Although we were Jewish, my parents were not Orthodox and we enjoyed a Christmas tree. We also celebrated the Feast of St. Nicholas in early December, and a switch was always put behind the mirror in our room the night before, in case we had been naughty and St. Nicholas, rather than leaving presents, would have to beat us instead. We learnt very early on that this switch was for show, but pretended fear just to keep our grown-ups happy.

I remember one morning when St. Nicholas left us a big bag with different packets of sweets. We each took our bag back into our beds – I to admire the wrappings and Stefan began to unwrap each sweet, take a bite and then rewrap the bitten item. Having gone through the whole lot in this fashion, he put them all back into the bag and beat it with his fist to make them large again. We still tease him about it.

All the grown-ups in our family worked very hard, but they were successful and up to the age of six, we children lived a structured, untroubled and protected life. However, we had to give as well as take. We were expected to behave and do as we were told. I cannot remember ever being hit; I think our punishment was more the withdrawal-of-approval-and-love type. We were enrolled in school in September 1938, but in the circumstances it never happened.

I suppose at this point I should go back a bit and put in what I know about my grandparents, both paternal and maternal.

I cannot really remember my paternal grandparents. My grandfather's name was Maximilian Popper and my grandmother's name was Anna (née Bender, also spelled Benda). They came from Bohemia and were married in Prague on 16th August 1896.

By the time my father was born they were living in Vienna, where my grandfather was, I seem to remember, a wine merchant, and my father used to tell us of his first day in primary school, when on giving his name to the teacher, he got the reply, "I know the Poppers – they come from Bohemia and are very cheeky." I can vaguely remember going to their flat and being entranced by their large Alsatian. My grandfather was killed soon after

A younger Anna Popper with children Martha and Franz Ferdinand
(Stefan and Lisa's father)

Austria's annexation by Germany[25] and my grandmother committed suicide
shortly thereafter by, I believe, jumping out of a fourth-floor window.[26]

My father also had a younger sister, and I hero-worshipped my Aunt
Martha. She was definitely a flapper: slim, cropped hair and a keen dancer
and socialiser. She was always very nicely dressed and I particularly admired
a small gold watch on a satin grosgrain ribbon which she wore on her wrist.

---

25 Lisa has this fact wrong as Maximilian Popper's death certificate shows he died
in 1936, long before the annexation.
26 What Lisa has written is what I too had understood, but the death certificate
shows an overdose of the barbiturate Veronal.

84

She married a German[27] non-Jew called Edgar Rehm; like my father a member of the legal profession. After the annexation, when it was strictly forbidden for non-Jews to be married to Jews, the two divorced and Aunt Martha went into hiding, with Edgar providing her with food and all the necessities of life. When he was called up this ceased, and at some stage during his several years of army service, knowing what was happening to the Jews, he remarried on the assumption that he had to be a widower.[28] In fact my aunt survived the war, badly wounded during an air raid (she was still in hiding and could not go to an air-raid shelter) and starving as she had no ration cards. Edgar and she were in touch after the war but the shock of his second marriage must have been severe and she did not long survive the end of the war.

It is strange twist of fate that her brother, my father, whom she did not see again in this life, died of a heart attack on his first visit to Vienna in 1956, and that they share a grave in the Zentralfriedhof in Vienna.

My maternal grandfather, Albert Waldmann – always called Bela – was born in Boesing, then in the Kingdom of Hungary, now Slovakia, on 18th September 1870. His father's name was Moses and his mother was Johana (née Bruner). My mother always told me that when Albert was thirteen he left for Vienna, journeying on foot to be apprenticed to a cabinetmaker. I cannot, of course, verify this, so my childhood memory has to suffice.

He was a tall, bald man with a very stern face, but very kind eyes. I was always a little afraid of him, but in my heart I knew that if I wanted something, I could always approach him.

My maternal grandmother Amalie Klug, always called Malie, was born in Sered, now Slovakia, on 29th December 1874. Her father's name was Leopold Klug and her mother was Regina (née Steiner). I do not know whether my grandmother went to Vienna on her own or with her parents; neither do I know what age she was when she got there. But again, based on what my mother told me she was running her own corsetry shop in Vienna, before the turn of the century.

My grandmother was short, unashamedly round and had a jovial

---

27 She means Austrian.

28 This account does not seem to be correct in the light of subsequent research. (see chapter 21) Uncle Edgar's remarriage is thought to have taken place in 1952.

Amelie Waldmann (née Klug)

manner. She had very well-defined features in a strikingly lovely face. She was always ready for a laugh and a sing-song and she was a very important person in my life.

They got married in Magyarfalva on 2nd May 1897, and as they were able to get out of Vienna in 1939 I have many happy memories of them, but more of that later.

As already mentioned, my father was born in Vienna on 11th September 1897 and was given the imposing name of Franz Ferdinand. He served in the Austrian Army during the First World War and spent time on the Russian Front. It was an experience which he, a keen spinner of yarns and teller of stories, never mentioned. He became a lieutenant in the reserve (No. 2297) on 1st December 1917 in the Infantry Regiment No. 4. He studied law and got his doctorate and licence to practise[29] in December MCMXX (1920). Like his sister, he enjoyed life in the Vienna of those days; he enjoyed the coffee houses, the music, the opera. He knew a lot of songs, and when we were far away from that lifestyle, Stefan and I learned and enjoyed extracts from all the liveliest operettas. He also studied Ancient Greek and was steeped in that mythology, which was another thing we were to learn about and enjoy in the future when life had changed completely. My father spoke several languages, but not English. This he had to rectify later.

My father was bald, of medium build and height, and for many years I thought that men with hair had something wrong with them. Throughout all the traumas that befell him and his family I can never remember him ever losing his joie de vivre, or his caring attitude towards us children. He made sure, as far as he was able, that we would not miss out either emotionally or intellectually on what we would have had, had we stayed in Vienna. I consider him to be one of the unsung heroes of this life.

My mother, Margarethe Waldmann, was born in Vienna on 11th January 1900 and was of a much more serious disposition than my father. She was brilliantly intelligent and was born ahead of her time. She told me that as a young woman she suffered from severe depression which she put down to being totally frustrated at having to live the narrow and unrewarding life that was then usual for a female in her circumstances. She did, however, rebel sufficiently to study astrology in the days when it was the brain and not a computer which did all the work, and this gave her something to occupy

---

29   His licence to practise came several years later.

her mind. She never had a real occupation and although she did help in the Kaffee Herrenhof, I do not think this satisfied her. She learned to drive, passing her driving test in the 1920s, and also studied English, in which she was quite fluent, a fact that was to stand us all in good stead when we fled Austria in 1938.

My mother was not very tall, with long, thick, dark brown hair and blue eyes. Unfortunately, she was very short-sighted so her eyes only came alive when she took her glasses off to inspect something very precisely at close range. In contrast to my father she did not like walking or any sort of exercise in fact, preferring to use her energy on quieter, more intellectual pursuits. She and I met very well in the sphere of the mind, but in the sphere of the heart we had major problems.

Her generation was definitely made of sterner stuff than we are. She had her tonsils out on the kitchen table without anaesthetic, just after the First World War ended in 1918, and really thought nothing of it.

She and my father married on the 3rd of June 1927 in the Muellnergasse 21, Vienna, and went to live at Rauhensteingasse No. 8.

The few people I have mentioned does not mean that we came from a small family. We were actually a very large tribe and I vaguely remember one of my uncles or great-uncles who owned a car allowing me to sit on his lap and turn the steering wheel. Most of this part of family died during the Holocaust, many making their journey to death via Theresienstadt concentration camp.

However, one of my grandmother's sisters, Cilka Koeppel, survived, being hidden by nuns in France right throughout the war. I never met her, neither do I remember her, but I know she lived her last few years in New York (some of the family having gone to the USA).

However, one other branch of the family managed to escape, and that was my mother's brother, Johannes (whom we always called Uncle Hans), his wife Edith (my favourite aunt) and their little girl – three years younger than us – called Franziska. The latter was joined by a little sister some years later, but I have no contact with her, presumably because her life experiences are completely different to mine. Unfortunately my uncle is now dead, but my aunt is still alive aged ninety-three and living in London.[30] They have been and still are my life's companions.

---

30   Edith Waldmann died in June 2008 aged 102.

Eigenhändige Unterschrift des Inhabers:

Margarethe Popper

Margarethe Popper – Driving licence

Franz Ferdinand and Margarethe

Uncle Hans was a gifted architect and mathematician and designed the interior of the Kaffee Herrenhof in beautiful Art Deco style. He and my Aunt Edith also owned a café called the Kaffee Josefstadt, and my aunt ran it while he worked at his profession.

Having introduced the family as far as I know it, let me now return to the spring of 1938.

It all happened very quickly. Three days after the annexation (I know this now), I was woken up by a lot of shouting, lights going on, heavy footsteps and the anxious voices of my parents. Our door was flung open but nothing else happened. The story of what really happened that night is explained in graphic detail in a statement my father put together after the war.

However, it is described very differently in a brief statement written by him and stamped by the Hitler Movement of the NSDAD Construction and Artisan Trades i.e.:

It is confirmed that a house search was undertaken at the home of Dr. Franz Ferdinand Popper, Wien 1, Rauhensteingasse 8, on 15.3.1938. With the exception of three pistols, which were voluntarily surrendered, the only money found belonged to clients and this was left in situ. An officer's sword belonging to the above named, as a one-time officer, was also left.

Unfortunately, the signature is illegible.

I can only remember odd events which occurred during the next few weeks and months.

I remember being chased away from somewhere in the park and our Detta[31] hurrying us home.

I can remember being in a room in the top of a tower in a large castle in the country and not being allowed to go out. I have found out since that this castle belonged to my mother's best friend, called Alice. I never did know her surname[32] and she took the risk of hiding us, but for how long and when I do not know.

According to my mother, Alice had an unusual life. As quite a young

---

31 I think this is a synonym for 'nanny', but it could be a name.
32 It was Fischer. I do not remember this or the preceding incident. I wonder if the former is the same incident I recount with me on the scooter and saluting the SA man.

woman she fell in love, but for some reason the romance did not end in marriage and she married someone else. Many years later, she met her original sweetheart, also married, and they decided that this time they would not lose each other again, got divorced and married each other. It was during Alice's second marriage that we were given shelter.

My father had viewed what was going on in Germany for some months and in 1937 he and my maternal grandparents had gone to what was then Palestine to see whether that was the place to flee to. On the way back, the ship docked in Larnaca, Cyprus for the day and they all got off and looked around. One day was enough: my father had made up his mind where he was going to take his family should the need arise. Even language was no problem here as he spoke Ancient Greek, not too dissimilar to the modern version, and my mother spoke English, the language of government in Cyprus.[33]

However, my father was a lawyer and this is a profession which can only be practised in the country where one is trained. So now, in 1938, he had to cast around for something to do that could be learnt quickly and which would earn money in any country. In the event he settled on confectionery production (after all, parents will always buy their children goodies to eat), and when we were back in our flat (when and for how long, I do not know), Stefan and I had a wonderful time tasting all the sweets that were being produced.

Another memory I have is of being taken somewhere, amidst huge crowds, and standing around for hours. I believe that it was the British Embassy and we were there either to see if we could get to England, or more likely to be baptised. There was still the hope extant then that if a Jew was baptised he would be safe from persecution. The above is an assumption, but from snippets of conversation I think I am pretty close to the truth.

Stefan and I were in real danger: twins were much wanted for medical experiments, and twins of different gender were thin on the ground.[34]

Besides all this, there was the everlasting and ever-increasing

---

33 I knew about the holiday but none of the other points which she makes, but it does not tie in with a previous initial application made by him to go to Australia.

34 Lisa is right about the risk for twins later on, but whether it was already a danger in 1938 I do not know but would be surprised. I also think identical twins were at greater risk.

officialdom to be dealt with. Receipts had to be obtained showing that there were no taxes outstanding, that the rent was paid up to date, that no cleaning bills were due, that nothing was known either against my father or my mother by the police and so on. It was bad enough obtaining these papers once, but they all had a life of only six weeks and as we did not leave until the end of August, i.e. over five months of Nazi occupation, they all had to be renewed. Drawing attention to oneself as a Jew was, at that time, not good practice. In fact I have one receipt which shows that rent was paid for August, September and October 1938, an indication of how important it was to give nothing away.

Besides this, there was a question of what to take of the items that were left, arranging for shipment etc., etc.

We children were obviously very aware of things happening and my parents were terrified that when out we would blab about going abroad. And this is where the bathing hut in Kritzendorf comes in.

Every morning when we visited my father, his stories would now start with the words, "Well, children, tomorrow we will go to Kritzendorf." And that, as far as we were concerned, was where we were going.

In fact, we went to the railway station one night. I thought it was about midnight, but it could just as easily have been eight, nine or ten o'clock. We still thought we were going to Kritzendorf, not having any idea of how one got there. But I did wonder, as my maternal grandparents and my Aunt Martha came to see us off and shed many tears. On leaving, Aunt Martha took off the gold watch I so admired and put it on my wrist – and I knew then that something terrible was happening.

We travelled by sleeper and when we woke up we found ourselves in Italy on the way to Trieste. As soon as we saw the sea Stefan was sick, although he was not sick on the boat. He too must have sensed the enormity of what was happening.

We were booked to travel on the Italian liner *Gerusalemme*. Our household effects were to travel on the same boat. I remember absolutely nothing about boarding or about the trip. Obviously I was not seasick because I think that would have stuck in my memory.

I also remember nothing of our arrival in Larnaca. My next memory is of us living in a cosy house at Kimon Street, Larnaca. Larnaca in those days was a sleepy little village with a wonderful palm-fringed seafront promenade, and we all went there every evening to meet other refugees and to enjoy a drink at the Four Lanterns Hotel.[35]

Our Austrian passports had a very short life left and in view of the fact that by this time Austria was part of Germany, my parents were issued with German passports by the German Consulate in Larnaca. My father's passport was No. 176, and my mother's (whose passport we children were on) was No. 175. We were considered to be enemy aliens and my parents had to go to the police station morning and evening to sign in. What evil the authorities thought they were going to do in the given circumstances is a riddle.[36]

Besides the settling-in process in very different circumstances to the ones in Vienna, two matters were pressing: earning a living and getting us to school. A third imperative turned up after we had been there only a few days, in that I became very ill. It was finally diagnosed as paratyphoid and, in those days, before antibiotics, it took several weeks before I was well again. It must have been a very anxious and difficult time for my parents.

When I was better I remember my father taking us for a walk along the pier, which I believe still exists – it was certainly there when I visited in 1992 – and Stefan got his foot caught between the planks.

I think we children must have been thoroughly traumatised, because I can remember him bursting into tears and crying, "I'll never get away from here, I'll never get away from here." Obviously he could and did.

As far as earning a living was concerned, we children were not aware of what was going on, but my father made his contacts and started making sweets in the kitchen of our house. I think his first selling forays were with a handcart.

And now the moment I dreaded most arrived: we were taken to school. I remember my father walking across what appeared to be a big field with us and leaving us at the American Academy, which was a co-educational school.

We were in a situation where we did not understand the language of instruction, which was English; neither could we talk to any of the children, who spoke Greek, Turkish and Armenian. I can remember nothing about

35 The hotel was there but my recollection is that it was the Sun Hall, but we could have been at both.
36 I think the attendance at the police station did not start in Larnaca but after release from detention, as mentioned by me.

the school, except that at playtime I learned to play marbles and a game with five stones, where first you had to throw one stone into the air and pick up one of the others before catching the airborne one, then throw it into the air again, twice this time, and pick up two stones during each throw, then three and one and then all four. I think I put all my energy into this game because I remember becoming quite good at it.

There were five sets of twins at the school during that year and we have a photograph of all of us, with Stefan and myself looking very worried.

However, all in all my memories of Larnaca are pleasant. My parents did their best to give us as normal a life as possible and we felt secure in our home.

Also at this time, my maternal grandparents and Uncle Hans, Aunt Edith and Franziska, known as Franzi, arrived from Vienna. I only have a copy of the Cyprus Certificate of Immigration (no. 227) which my father sent to my grandparents. This was issued on 18th January 1939 and remained valid for one year. It states that the persons named on the reverse were to take it to the British Consul in Vienna (Cyprus was a British Crown Colony at that time) together with their passports and a document proving their identity and suitability as immigrants to Cyprus. It also had to be certified by a notary public in Vienna and this was done on 27th January 1939 by Dr Erwin Herlinger. I must assume that a similar document existed for my uncle, aunt and cousin.[37] I do not remember my grandparents in Larnaca,[38] though no doubt they stayed with us, but I do remember my uncle and aunt and one memorable night in particular.

My parents had gone out (I believe it was their first outing in Cyprus) and we were left in my uncle and aunt's care. Unfortunately, I woke up and became absolutely hysterical, screaming for my parents without pause until they came home. I know I was no one's favourite that night.

My uncle, who, as an architect with engineering training, could practise his profession, got a job with a mining company and they, together with my grandparents, moved to the north coast of Cyprus to a place called

---

37 I think this is unlikely. I think they, like us, came with a tourist visa. We got the authorisation for the grandparents after we had obtained permanent residence and were able to sponsor them.

38 That is because we were in Platres when they arrived and never returned to live in Larnaca.

Polis Chrysochous. Life there was very primitive with no running water or sewerage. At that time Polis was a tiny village, in the centre of which stood (and still stands) a very old olive tree, which is at least eight hundred years old. My Aunt Edith still remembers sitting around that tree in the evenings with the local doctor and I presume others of the village community.

As far as we were concerned, either the business was not going well or the heat was too much, but in the summer of 1939 we moved to the mountain resort of Platres. As we were enemy aliens,[39] this meant getting official permission for the move and a trip to the police station in Platres.

Platres is still a beautiful place and now, as then, it only has three main roads, the names of which are self-explanatory, i.e. Lower Road, Middle Road and Upper Road. My parents rented a house in, I think, Middle Road, which they ran as a coffee shop. As my mother could bake very well, Stefan and I enjoyed lots of bowl-licking.

The house was built into the mountain, surrounded by forest and with beautiful views. My father had a space next to the house cleared as a playground for us. We also got a swing on which, if we swung very hard, we could just get over the edge of the clearing.

And thus began the most idyllic summer any child could wish for. Platres in those days was absolutely safe, which meant that we were free to roam anywhere. At that time, the rainy season (which in Cyprus is during the winter months) was much more intense than it is now, and all the roads had little streams running along on either side. We paddled through these with bare feet on hot summer days and when pushed, drank too; the water was clear and tasty.

The Greek Cypriots love children and were quite amenable to the two of us – three sometimes as we had another girl, Elfie, whose parents were also refugees, as a playmate – appearing at their doors and asking for a glass of water or a piece of bread. Most of the houses were built into the hillside with flat roofs, which in late summer were covered by grapes drying into raisins, and no one minded us helping ourselves to some. In early summer, we had, of course, also helped ourselves to grapes.

My father arranged donkey and mule rides for us. Stefan and I usually rode together, with him in front. Most of the rides were great fun, but on

---

39 We certainly were classed as aliens and needed to register, but we could not
     have been classed as 'enemy' until after the declaration of war in September.

one occasion the saddle started slipping, and as Stefan saw a heap of stones ahead, he decided to throw himself off before we reached that obstacle and fell off perforce. I could not see anything but as I was holding on to him I fell off too and was very displeased. After that, when we did ride, we rode on our own.

There was one incident which I did not fully comprehend so the telling may be a little confused. I seem to remember a pit dug in the back yard, which somehow was to be used for winemaking. This pit was uncovered and one morning we awoke to the pitiful howling of a dog. On investigation, we saw a rather large mongrel which had fallen into the pit. My father could not get him out as the dog was afraid. The owner was finally found after enquiries at the local shop and he arrived, looking very angry. I do not know whether he was Greek or Turkish, but he was wearing the big, baggy black trousers that so many Cypriot men wore then. The dog was obviously pleased to see him and, what with him bending down and the animal leaping up, the rescue was effected. My father, who loved animals, was very pleased at this happy outcome, but then, to his horror, the owner took his belt off as though to beat the dog. There was one of those motionless moments when everyone froze and then the owner put the belt round the dog as a lead. What a relief! The dog had a quick drink, the pit was filled in and that was the end of the winemaking.

However, all good things must come to an end. There was no school in Platres, so we had to leave. This time we moved to Nicosia, and again my parents had to report their move to the police. On the 11th October 1939, my mother is shown as residing in Victoria Street, Nicosia. Unfortunately, I do not have any documents for my father.

We were now in the middle of town. The house was a large two-storey house, with a flagged hall which led right through to the back garden. The two doors were usually kept open to provide air, and in the evenings everyone sat either just inside or just outside the front door to see the world go by and to chat to friends and neighbours. The house stood on a corner and right opposite was the mosque – we were in the Turkish quarter. This was in the days when the muezzin called his congregation to prayer personally. At first it was very disturbing, but in no time at all it acquired all the comfortable familiarity of a loudly ticking clock.

My favourite place was the garden, which was walled, with a wonderful old tree (it may have been an olive tree) which had branches extending over the wall. I spent a lot of time in this tree, my own secret place for watching the world go by and calling out to friends.

My grandparents came to stay with us and my parents also let a room to another refugee couple called Weidmann, who had a sixteen-year-old son named Eric. We treated him as one of the adults and left him severely alone. I seem to recall quite a few refugee families living around us and I remember a Mr Kahn visiting my father when he suffered a bad attack of sciatica.

It was while at this house that Stefan and I were often taken to the local Turkish baths by the neighbours. I certainly enjoyed these trips.

The other really memorable thing that happened here is that I learned to read German. My parents had brought quite a few books with them, for us and for them, and used to read ours aloud every evening (no radio for enemy aliens, and TV did not exist). Of course, all these books were in Gothic print. While ill, I decided that I wanted to read on my own and my grandfather was delegated to teach me. I remember him coming up to our room (Stefan and I both had jaundice), and after having ascertained that my grandfather (whom we called Opapa, my grandmother being Omama) had brought his glasses with him, we opened the book and to his astonishment I proceeded to 'read'. What I had kept very quiet was that I knew all the stories by heart, so my achievement was astonishing but illusory. Another book was brought that I had not memorised and I now went through all the agonies of any child learning to master the art of reading. Stefan was taught to read at the same time, but I do not think he liked it as much as I did.

However, it was not just we children who were immersed in learning. Opapa decided that he had to learn English. So at sixty-eight and with just the local English rag (which even now contains some horrendous mistakes) and a very old dictionary which he had brought with him from Vienna, he taught himself English. He learned to read quite fluently but had great difficulty speaking, as he never heard the language.

I have no real recollection of my grandmother at this period, probably because I was too busy learning to be an independent individual.

And now I come to what to me was the most dreaded of all things: school. My mother was adamant that we were to go to a school near home and the nearest was a Roman Catholic convent, St. *Joseph's*, where the tuition was in French. Again we were faced with another language – we had picked up some Greek by this time, but were expected to speak French at school. I learned nothing here, not even any games with marbles or stones. In fact, I disliked this school intensely; it was much too rigid and structured for me, and I managed to produce a daily headache, fact not fiction, which kept me away from it for long periods of time. The headache always disappeared halfway through the morning and I was then free to climb my tree and read German.

In the meantime my parents were back in the sweet-production mode. This time they went for more exotic items such as chocolates, and I remember that the packaging of these caused some problems as they wanted these good-quality items in nice-looking boxes. In the end they found another refugee lady, whose name I cannot remember, who hand-painted pictures of rather Rubenesque ladies and these were stuck onto the boxes.

We children were never burdened with any grown-up problems, but children do pick up vibes and it seemed to me that my parents were making ends meet and life was tolerable.

Summer 1940 approached with the promise of intense heat. In those days refrigerators were as rare as hens' teeth and freezers were unknown. However, as the temperature stayed well over 100 degrees Fahrenheit for months on end, large blocks of ice were delivered. These were put into a metal container. I cannot remember whether the latter had a tap to let off the water or whether this had to be scooped out, but one could keep perishables cool in this way. Shopping for meat and vegetables was done on a daily basis, usually by a trip to the market. It was always my grandmother who did this, and I believe she also did the cooking. One usually had an order book for the grocer, wrote into it one's requirements, dropped it off at the shop and the goods were delivered and paid for later on in the day. It would have been much easier with a phone, but this again was a rare and expensive luxury out of most people's reach.

Kitchens were extremely primitive. No running hot water (it had to be boiled as and when required), and no oven, just two Primuses which we lit with the local drink ouzo, as it was much cheaper than spirits and worked just as well. On thinking back, it amazes me what wonderful meals my grandmother managed to turn out in such basic surroundings. She had the added burden of having to cook separately for my grandfather, who had diabetes and whose food had to be weighed out carefully.

In that heat, drinking sufficient water was a matter of need and comfort, but all water had to be boiled and then cooled,[40] and with so many people in the family, plus cooking and preparing special meals for my grandfather, the Primuses were in constant use and the kitchen always very hot.

Water was not always plentiful and this too was delivered to the house, unless one was lucky enough to have a well, which was usually several miles away in the countryside. In the latter case, the water container was filled up by hand-pumping whenever the necessity arose. Our house in Victoria Street did not have a pump, so water was on occasion delivered.[41]

But lurking in the background was the fact that we were enemy aliens, and on the 12th June 1940 all the men were interned. It was not an arduous internment, in fact the location was very pleasant, given that it was now very hot in Nicosia. The men were sent to Prodromos, the highest village in Cyprus, and were accommodated in the Berengaria Hotel, a large stone-built edifice which stood on a hill and dominated the tiny village. As an aside, the Berengaria is now derelict and I believe is to be pulled down.

Needless to say, this caused another huge family upheaval. The house in Victoria Street was vacated and we moved to Prodromos. I am not sure whether we took everything with us or if some of the items were stored in Nicosia. One must bear in mind that all this had to be accomplished without telephones or cars. Handwritten notes or personal visits were the means of communication, and walking or the use of local buses or lorries were the means of transport.

My mother is shown as having registered at the police station *in Prodromos on 2nd August 1940*. Although this must have caused my parents terrible problems, it gave us children another summer of total freedom in the mountains. The house we took, which Stefan, his wife Wendy and I found on a trip to Prodromos in January 1999, stood as I remember it, overlooking the main village which lies in a shallow valley, facing west towards another mountain range. On the other side across the valley floor we could see the Berengaria Hotel.

---

40 I do not remember this happening, though it was what occurred later in Africa.

41 As Victoria Street was in town it may have had a mains supply. I remember nothing of any of this.

The house had a large balcony off the first floor and we sat there every evening and watched the sun go down – this was always spectacular. Stefan had one corner of the balcony where he kept all his treasures and played. Of course, these were boy's treasures, so I never went near them, but he remembers being very happy there.

The house had no electricity and I am not sure whether it had running water and sewerage. We used oil lamps, which gave a wonderfully gentle glow after the sun had gone down. I remember clearly helping my grandmother to fill these lamps and to clean the glass cylinders.

Just as I have no recollection of my grandmother in Victoria Street, so here I have absolutely no recollection of my mother, but lots of memories of my grandmother. When we were doing the lamps or I was helping her in some other way, she sang folk songs to me, made jokes and generally appeared to be happy, which I found very reassuring.

Every morning the children of the refugee families (Prodromos was full of families who had followed their men) trooped over to the Berengaria to visit our respective fathers and then to sit with my father and listen to him recount the tales of Greek mythology. We could not have had a better setting. The hotel had a huge balcony at the back, surrounded by quite a thick forest, and we listened entranced. Each of us had our favourites, and every time my father finished a story he was overwhelmed by a shouting horde all asking for their favourite tale.

At lunchtime we went home and in the afternoon, the grown-ups accompanied us back to the hotel. The roads were non-existent so everyone made sure to walk back in daylight, and this was very important to me because I did not want to miss the sunsets.

When Stefan, Wendy and I were in Prodromos in January 1999, we actually drove down to the village and did not see a single shop, just three or four very narrow, very steep streets, bordered by very decrepit houses which were, however, all inhabited. It made me wonder where and how my grandmother did the shopping.[42]

The men were interned until October 1940, when we returned to Nicosia. This time we moved into a very old part of Nicosia, an area of narrow

---

42   There was and is a coffee shop and I think general store on the road leading from the house to the Berengaria. The road at this point is fairly level so I suspect that was where she went.

streets and mostly single-storey dwellings. This is now a conservation area and lies just inside the old city walls, near the Famagusta Gate. Nicosia was a walled city and had two other gates, the Paphos Gate and the Kyrenia Gate. Besides the walls it also had a wide moat which is now used for car parking, open-air coffee shops etc., etc.

Although this is really outside the scope of this story I feel I must give some brief notes on the Famagusta Gate, which is the most impressive of the three. It was built by the Venetians and originally called Porta Giuliana after Count Giulio Savorgnano, who built the walls in 1567. The Turks called it 'That-el-kaleh', which I believe means 'lower fortress'. The gate has a vaulted passage and a spherical dome (almost eleven metres in diameter) in the centre of this archway. Today the Famagusta Gate, together with its adjacent six hundred-seat open-air theatre in the moat, is the cultural centre of the Nicosia municipality. The Famagusta Gate is relatively young in Cypriot terms. The history of Cyprus goes back an authenticated eight thousand years.

Our address was Chrysaliniotissa Street No. 9, and my mother is shown as having been registered at this address on 28th April 1941. I know, however, that we came here in the autumn of 1940, because we spent the winter in yet another school (more of that later).

Our house here had a wide marbled hall, going from the front door to the back garden, and as in Victoria Street the doors were not shut during the day to keep the air circulation going. There was a large room on either side of the hall, each with windows onto the street, and the kitchen, toilet etc. were extended into the back garden. As was and is still customary in Cyprus, everyone sat either inside or outside their front door in the evenings and as there was no traffic, Stefan and I, together with all the local children, played hopscotch and spinning tops (at which both of us became quite adept) out in the street. Stefan had a scooter at that time, which he loved, and when it came to racing around he did his on wheels, not on legs as the rest of us did.

I got very friendly with all the neighbours, and used to sit with them and watch them make lace, not with bobbins but with needles. I always admired their lovely work. My Greek was nowhere near good enough to understand their conversations but I felt at ease in their circle.

To my mother's horror I was accepted to such an extent that they frequently took me to the Greek Orthodox church which stood at the end of the road, and where I enthusiastically kissed all the icons, without any idea of why. This church called Chrysaliniotissa is one of the oldest churches in Nicosia and well worth a visit.

We had our dining table in the hall, and to our delight a swallow built its nest under the central beam and in due course produced some young. We used to watch her swooping in and out with food for her brood. It was in this house that Stefan and I were given a chicken each – his was Hansel and mine was Gretel, as in the fairy tale, but in fact Hansel was a she and laid eggs as well as Gretel. We loved these animals.

At this time the Germans were bombing Crete and my father felt that we should have a bomb shelter dug in the garden. This was duly done and kitted out with water, some food and a couple of camp beds. It was covered with, I think, corrugated iron and then with several feet of soil. The whole thing was surrounded by trees.

Two things make this shelter memorable. The first one concerns Stefan, who was leaping off it one afternoon. His leaps got more and more daring until he leapt straight into the branches of a tree and scratched his face quite badly. He did not want my mother to know and so, to make himself inconspicuous, hung his pillowcase over his face. We spent a long time laughing during that evening meal.[43]

The other memory concerns one of the few times when we heard an air-raid siren go off. As I have already said, doors were always kept open and before we could gather ourselves together the entire neighbourhood was in the shelter with no space for us.

And now for that most dreaded subject: school. Again, my mother wanted us to be as close to home as possible and so this year we went to a Greek school. We both found this quite comfortable, in fact; firstly because we could now communicate in that language, and secondly because we knew all the important games played during break times, i.e. marbles, five stones, spinning tops and hopscotch. Again, I cannot remember learning anything, but I enjoyed myself.

We had just settled comfortably when, in early June 1941, we were told that all English families and Jewish refugees were to be evacuated. I think we were given about one week's notice and told that we could only

---

43 I cannot remember this at all; I must have been successful in blotting it out of my memory!

take what we could carry. We were not, of course, told where we would be going.

Deciding what to take must have been a real problem. After all, Stefan and I were just nine and not able to carry very much. I believe that the neighbours came up trumps and stored a lot of our things. This was an act of faith as no one knew whether we would be back. In the event, when we did eventually come back in May 1947, most of our things were returned to us.

The thing that really upset Stefan and me was having to have Hansel and Gretel killed – no one wanted them. They were prepared for cooking and given away. None of us had the heart to eat our pets.

At that time Cyprus had a very short railway line from Nicosia to Famagusta, on which ran a small wood-fired train. On the due date we got onto this train with Stefan carrying my mother's portable typewriter, with great difficulty, I may say. I had managed to get tonsillitis, so besides carrying practically nothing I was also ill.

We got to Famagusta at around lunchtime, I believe, and boarded a ship – Stefan and I thought it was all great fun. No one knew where we were going, or whether the journey would be through safe or dangerous waters. We went to bed that night and the next day, again about lunchtime, found ourselves coming into port. We had been taken to Haifa in what was then Palestine. I have a copy of the temporary residence permit which was issued to my father by the inspector of migration in Haifa on 12th June 1941.

We were put onto buses, amidst typical Middle Eastern chaos, and finished up in Tel Aviv. I do not remember whether we were allocated our quarters immediately or whether we spent a night or two in some reception centre, but I know we finished up living in one ground-floor room, with a fairly large veranda. The room was about five minutes' walk from the beach and we spent a lot of time there. Tel Aviv was obviously considered safe, as Stefan and I were sent out to do the shopping.

I don't know how my parents supported us all at this time; whether they had savings, or whether they got an allowance. What I do remember is that we were very short of money and that chocolate (bearing in mind that we were very spoiled when it came to sweets) was doled out at a rate of one square per day. I managed to be ill with monotonous regularity, usually with tonsillitis.

There are several things I remember. One is that our landlady had a gramophone and my father used to dance with me, which I loved. I also had my first perm here, as my mother considered that my baby-fine hair always looked a mess.

These are the nice memories. Now for the bad ones.

I had toothache and was taken to the dentist, who said that I would have to have a tooth out. I was terrified. As he approached with his hypodermic, I leaped out of the chair, ran through the door and stayed away until it was dark. Again, I was nobody's favourite that evening and had to put up with the toothache, which, as it was a baby tooth, was not too critical.

The next unpleasant thing that happened was that one evening when we children were out with our father, I suddenly felt an intense pain in my eye. I screamed loudly (I was pretty good at that) and said that I could not see. My father rushed me into the nearest shop, which by sheer chance was a chemist, and it was established that something had got stuck in my eye and caused a cut. The chemist assured my father that the rather large red mark on the white of the eye would fade. We never did discover what it was, but my father surmised that it might have been someone's long fingernail at the end of a swinging arm.

Our stay in Palestine was not happy; not that our parents ever said anything to us, but I felt their frustration at not having anything to do (how often can one go to the beach without getting bored?) and not daring to start anything as we had been told that we would only get twenty-four hours' notice before leaving. This latter was a real burden, because it meant that we literally lived out of suitcases for just over five months. Also, as we all shared a room, there was a distinct lack of privacy. My mother hated the room, as we got quite a few cockroaches, which I was delegated to kill – not my favourite job.

We left Palestine on 25th November 1941 and again I was ill with tonsillitis and quite a high temperature. I seem to remember waiting around and getting onto buses which took us to a station from where we were to go to, I believe, Port Said,[44] to board a ship to who knew where.

The train was very crowded and we had quite a job finding a seat. My mother finally spied two seats in a compartment (we were travelling on

---

44   I think initially we went to Cairo and then travelled on.

a corridor train), only to be told by one of the German refugees – a Mrs Helft,[45] who had a daughter, Dorothy, slightly younger than us – that we could not take up the space, as I was ill. My mother made very short work of her and we sat down. I think my father and Stefan were either standing or in another compartment.

On arrival at the port, we saw a large ship whose top two or three decks were crowded with soldiers; in other words, we were to travel on a troop carrier.

We were a large, unwieldy crowd and it took us a long time to board as we were gradually funnelled into a single line and had to register with an official. Over his table was a large notice saying that there was to be no fraternising, and this was repeated on all the decks. However, *the best laid plans of mice and men gang aft agley...*

Among our group there was a German family called Schlochauer; a father, mother and two beautiful daughters, Helga, aged about eighteen, and Meta, about sixteen.

From the top decks a young lieutenant picked Helga out and said to his mate, "I will be engaged to that one before we dock", and so he was. We got this story from her parents, when we met them again years later in Cyprus.

I am not sure on which deck we ended up but I don't think it was too far down. I was instantly put to bed and so missed all the fun of leaving port. In those days one stayed in bed until one's immune system overcame the illness and my mother, just to make sure, insisted on bed rest for one whole day without a temperature before one was allowed to get up. My tonsillitis seemed to take a long time to clear up, and to stop me complaining about being bored, I was given two German books to read, both heavy tomes. The first was Gibbon's *The Decline and Fall of the Roman Empire* and the second a collection of Indian folklore. I understood the individual words but got only about 10% of the sense of the stories, which maybe was just as well.

I was finally allowed up and enjoyed playing with the other children on deck.

We approached a harbour on 17th December 1941, but because the ship was large, we had to land by tender. This meant going down a swaying ladder and my cousin, Franzi, only just five, got her hand caught between

---

45   This is the same lady I have referred to as Heald.

the ladder rail and the ship and lost a fingernail. She cried horribly and getting her hand dressed was top priority when we finally reached terra firma. It was at this stage that we found out that we were now in Dar es Salaam in the then Tanganyika territory, now Tanzania.

Each head of family was given a rail ticket and some money and off we went to the station – again in buses. We found that our destination was to be Tabora, the place where Stanley is supposed to have met Livingstone with the famous words, "Dr Livingstone, I presume."[46] We were told that the journey would take just over two days.

The train was a pleasant surprise. The compartments (again we were on a corridor train) consisted of four bunks, the top ones being folded down during the day. These bunks were made up as beds at night. There was a restaurant car, which served what to us seemed good and plentiful food, and we settled down for the trip.

The train was, I believe, wood-fired and chugged through the shrub and bush at a leisurely pace. The rails had lots of curves and at night it was lovely to see the lighted carriages ahead and behind, with the snorting engine spewing out sparks into the dark and mysterious landscape. We spent a lot of time looking out during the day in the hope that we would see some wildlife, but alas, saw nothing.

We stopped at various small stations, where the platforms, level with the rails, were always awash with people of all shapes, ages and sizes, selling anything from food to carved wooden figures. The only station of any consequence whose name I remember was Dodoma, where we got off and walked among the crowds. Stefan and I were to get to know Dodoma very well indeed, but that was all in the future.

Eventually, just as we were all getting very fed up with promenading up and down the length of the train, we got to Tabora. We were met by yet more officialdom, put into a taxi and taken to the house which had been allocated to us. The address was in an area called Rufita. At some stage we moved to another house where, except for a stay of a few months in Kigoma on the shores of Lake Tanganyika (more of that later), we stayed until our departure on 10th April 1947.[47]

Besides the house, which was lightly furnished and contained just

---

46 Actually Ujiji, near Kigoma. I think Livingstone's heart is buried near Tabora.
47 We actually moved several times in Tabora as I can remember several houses we lived in, though not in detail.

enough food to keep us going until the next day, we found that we had to have at least one houseboy, always called 'boy'; one cook, always called '*mpishi*', the Swahili for 'cook'; and one young lad to do all the running around for the other two, always called '*mtoto*', the Swahili for 'child'. Suitable candidates were to be sent around the next day. If possible, one also had to have someone to do the laundry, but we could not afford this on the allowance we were getting (*£26 per month*[48]) and so the 'boy' and the *mtoto* had to perform this daily ritual.

The kitchen was always a separate building, quite a few steps from the main house, and the cooking was done on a very temperamental wood-fired range. The *mpishi* usually did the shopping as he got much better deals than my mother, and even so probably did very well out of it. We got a rather older *mpishi* who was actually quite a good cook.

Even so, we did go into the main part of the village the next day and found a general store run by a Mr Patel, which seemed to have everything from hardware to cloth. If Mr Patel did not have it, he was able to get it within a few days. I hated the heat and would only walk in the afternoons.

The house had a corrugated iron roof and, during the rainy season, when the rain just came down like stair rods, the sound on the roof was like a wild drumming. It was very cosy to curl up in bed under a mosquito net at such times. Mosquito nets were essential, as were screens on all the doors and windows. In the evening, one covered one's arms and legs, but nevertheless got bitten. The screens were covered by a variety of lizards, both inside and out, which ate bugs to their hearts' content.

If one became ill, it was automatically assumed that one had malaria and, as a matter of course, a blood slide was taken. This meant a prick in the fingertip and I was absolutely terrified of becoming ill and having to face a needle. But, true to form, I was the first one in the family to get a temperature and the doctor duly arrived. He approached my bed with his needle and small glass plate and I let him get just near enough to be within kicking distance, when I let fly.

He was not at all amused and, as he glared at me from the doorway, minus a sample of blood, he said to my mother, "I hope she dies of blackwater fever, but give her two quinine a day anyway."

---

48   That is my computation from the documents I have seen.

My mother was furious at my behaviour and no one was allowed to speak to me until I got better. I wrote to my grandmother about this and said defiantly that I enjoyed the company of my books.

Quite soon after arriving in Tabora, we got a kitten, whom we christened Peter and all loved madly. One morning he did not come home and my father found his body on the road – he had been attacked by something bigger. We were all devastated, and it was the only time in my life that I saw my father cry. My grandparents, uncle, aunt and Franziska had been sent to a real one-horse place called Nzega, where there was employment for my uncle. I believe there were only two other European families there and my grandparents must have felt like fish out of water, as they did not speak English.

It was the locals' habit to address the lady of the house with a watered-down version of the word 'memsahib', abbreviated to 'mama', and I believe that my grandmother was most insulted at this form of address when she first heard it.

She told us that she rounded on the poor boy and said to him in German, "I am not your mama." The fact that she spoke German had a strong effect as Tanganyika had been under German rule until the end of the First World War; that is, 1918, and at that time there was still a healthy respect for German-speakers.

Letters between my grandparents and my mother and myself (I had to put in my tuppence' worth) were exchanged frequently and I believe they were carried on lorries that drove between Tabora and all the other places on a daily basis.

Tabora had a Roman Catholic mission and I remember that one afternoon we all trooped over there. It was built in the hacienda style and we sat surrounded by lovely plants scrambling over the veranda rails. We met one old nun, who had come to Tanganyika at the turn of the century and had walked from Dar es Salaam to Tabora, where she had remained. I was very impressed. The nuns were very friendly and gave us children a drink of buttermilk, which I had never had before. It was cold and delicious.

In the letters previously mentioned, there was a lot of talk about getting work – who had it, who was getting it, what they were paid and so on – but in fact my father was unemployed until 13ᵗʰ August 1942, at which time he got a job running a section of an Italian prisoner-of-war camp. He got this job mainly[49] because he spoke Latin, which enabled him to learn Italian practically overnight.

The camp was surrounded by stripped, pointed wooden stakes, about ten feet high and about six to nine inches apart. Imagine our amazement when many of them sprouted after having been in the soil for about a year. In fact, the soil was fantastically prolific and one could have vegetables for the table within four weeks of planting.

Most of the Italians were anything but professional soldiers, and as the war progressed and they were given a little freedom and allowed to go out, their warmth and culture was very much felt and appreciated in the community.

As far as Stefan and I were concerned, there was always the little matter of school. We were by now nine-and-a-half and totally uneducated. We knew that we would have to go to a boarding school, and I mention Arusha School, the one we actually went to, in a letter to my grandmother dated 2nd January 1942.

I am not sure when we actually left, but our first report relates to the second term of the school year 1941–1942. For some reason the school insisted on calling them 'terminal' reports.

Up till now, we had been very protected and had remained children, but Arusha, which lay in Masai country, at the foot of Mount Meru and within sight of Mount Kilimanjaro (which is perpetually covered in snow), was to have a profound effect on us. It was a co-educational boarding school and it took two days of travel for us to get there. Once there, we were on our own: there was no telephone, only letters which took days, and in an emergency a telegram. There was usually a group of children who did the journey together, and different mothers took it upon themselves to accompany us.

The first day of the journey was spent on the train to Dodoma, where we overnighted in the Dodoma Hotel, both going to school and coming back home. This hotel, as I remember it, had lots of corridors and external doors that were kept open during the night to cool the place down. I remember distinctly hyenas howling along these, a very scary experience, especially the first time. Dodoma was also overrun

---

49 Not sure about the reason as others had also got similar jobs, presumably without Latin.

by scorpions and I was much more terrified of these than I was of the hyenas.

The next part of the trip was done on the back of an open lorry. It was only about 274 miles, but due to the appalling roads it took all day. We all had to wear topis as otherwise we would have all died of sunstroke. About halfway, we entered – or departed, depending on whether we were coming or going – a tsetse fly area and the lorry was driven into a shed with us still on it and heavily doused with Flit and DDT. Thank goodness we had good immune systems.

Our journey to Arusha took us through the Serengeti Wild Animal Reserve and we all waited for this part of the journey. We saw huge herds of zebras and wildebeest, giraffes eating elegantly off the tops of shrubby trees and, best of all, lion families.

When we arrived at Arusha that first time, the boys and girls were separated. The girls' building was very modern with lots of windows. One entered into a wide hall, and off to the left were three rooms reserved for teachers. To the right was a flight of stairs which brought one into a corridor, off which were six dormitories. The entrances to each of the latter were open and had no doors. Directly opposite these openings were parallel openings which brought one onto an internal corridor where the prefects slept. Each dormitory had either six beds, when each bed had its small cupboard standing beside it, or five beds, when the five cupboards were joined up and stood together against a wall, with a bed at either end and three beds opposite. All the floors were parquet.

At the end of the outside corridor there was a further flight of stairs up and a repetition of the ground floor. Behind these stairs there was another small room. If, instead of turning right in the entrance hall, one walked straight on, one came to the toilets, a large locker room, a bathroom with eight handbasins (four and four standing back to back), and four bathrooms-cum-showers.

The gardens round the building were awash with canaas,[50] lilies and all sorts of other exotic plants. We had three giant tortoises in the grounds and they seemed to love our front garden. At night, the gardens were alive with fireflies, flying ants, lizards and no doubt scorpions and snakes, but we did not think about the latter. All sorts of exciting and mysterious sounds fired

---

50   I am not sure what she means – perhaps carnations?

our imagination, the most exciting being the drum with which messages were passed across vast distances.

The Masai looked very different to the Bantu people whom we had met in Tabora. They were slim and tall with aquiline features. They counted their wealth in cattle and still drank blood from the latter by puncturing a blood vessel in the neck. In fact they lived on blood, milk and meat – so much for vegetables. The women had short hair and wore lots of necklaces, and both sexes wore ear ornaments which hung from hugely enlarged lobes, some reaching to the shoulder.

The rite of passage from boy to man involved the individual having to kill a lion with a spear, and often this battle involved the death of the youth. I believe that when we were there this practice was already outlawed but still sometimes practised.

The young men had long hair which they covered in red ochre, and were wrapped in hides. Unfortunately, all their beauty was spoiled by the fact that they did not wash and smeared themselves with fat. But if one stood upwind and saw one standing tall and upright, holding a spear, it was a sight worth seeing.

There were several refugee children who travelled from Tabora with us, but I cannot remember who escorted us. They were Erna and Albert Schacht, both older than us, Erna being almost seventeen; Beatrice Gruenwald, younger than us and always known as Ulli or Trixie; Liselotte and Paul Heim, Liselotte being about fifteen and Paul about our age; Peter and Lisa Hoffer, Peter being our age and Lisa younger; and for just a term or two, Rolf and Vera Dessauer. Rolf was almost eighteen and Vera sixteen. Vera became a junior teacher – a teacher's assistant, one would call her now – after about a year. Dorothy Helft, a little younger than us and already mentioned in connection with her mother and the train compartment on the way to Port Said, came a few terms later.

We were all put into a six-bed dormitory, and given strict instructions not to speak German. In view of the fact that this was the only language which we knew really well, this instruction was naturally disobeyed.

We liked our beds, which were like mini four-posters, with a mosquito net suspended at the four corners. The next morning we were thrown into the routine as much by pushing and shoving as by verbal instruction. The wake-up bell sounded at about half past six, when everyone leapt out of bed, untucked their mosquito net and threw it over the top, which enabled us to turn the bed back completely. Then bathroom, get dressed, make bed and off along a covered way to the main building, where the boys were housed, to breakfast. The children sat at long tables, each headed by one of the teachers, who I will introduce later. Our days were always very regulated, but each headmaster (and we had four during the five years we were there) had his own pet foibles, so the rules varied under each regime. The prefects, little tin gods, sat at the head table with the headmaster.

Because of our age, Stefan and I were put into Standard 3. The age range at the school ran from seven to eighteen, as it did in the only other school for European children, which was situated in a place called Mbeya. This large age range posed huge discipline problems, especially as we were co-educational.

During the first few weeks, just keeping up with the daily routine and lessons took up all my time, but gradually people, both teachers and pupils, began to come into focus.

Our teachers, I think now, were the detritus of war. We had mainly women teachers, many of whom had come out to Africa as missionaries and then, through force of circumstances, found themselves co-opted into teaching in one or other of the two schools for European children.

Of the teachers who I can remember by name, two were from England, as was the nursing sister. One was Mrs Horne, middle-aged and nondescript, who was Standard 3's form mistress; and the other was Miss Wylie, who had studied art and therefore organised all the amateur dramatics. Sister Carter ruled the hospital and dispensary with a rod of iron and no one ever dared make a fuss about anything.

Mrs Horne had a pet monkey, which I hated as it was allowed to roam through the girls' building with impunity. It had the awful habit of leaping onto one's mosquito net and using it as a toilet. That was what I counted against Mrs Horne; what I liked about her was that she was very patient with us when we couldn't understand what she was saying, and best of all, for English literature she read *The Water-Babies* to us. I soon learned to follow and this story has always had a special meaning for me. We never found out how Mrs Horne came to be at the school, but I don't think she was ever a missionary.

Miss Wylie was a tall, big woman and wore her dark hair in a bob. She seemed terribly old to me, but she was probably in her thirties. Once I had got over my fear of her (she had a loud voice), I realised how kind she was. Miss Wylie had been a missionary.

Sister Carter was tall and spare, always immaculately dressed in white with a starched headdress. Our hospital-cum-dispensary was down a footpath, well trodden by many fearful feet. There were always Masai sitting beside the path, and very early on I saw one of them cutting off a piece of his toe with a razor blade. I was horrified, and on enquiring was told that he probably had a jigger; more of those little pests later.

I got to know the hospital pretty well because I continued to be ill at regular intervals, either with tonsillitis or malaria. I had got over my fear of blood slides by this time and, once ensconced in bed, quite enjoyed myself, as the hospital had a whole room full of books, which I devoured. There was one author in particular who wrote about schoolgirls, called Angela Brazil, whose books I particularly enjoyed.

Most of the rest of our women teachers were from Australia. There was Miss Newell, also tall and big and very heavily built, with her light brown hair tied back in a bun. She had been a missionary. She too was in her thirties but I cannot remember her ever taking us for any lessons.

Then there was Miss Latimer, small and sparrow-like, who, unfortunately for her, was the butt of all our pranks, and also an ex-missionary. On thinking back, she was one of those people who was a natural victim.

Then Miss Long, whose name suited her perfectly. Again I have no recollection of her ever taking us for any lessons.

We had another Australian teacher who was our games mistress – short hair and very butch, but I cannot remember her name. She took us for hockey, netball and basketball, and as she made up the rules as we went along this led to some incidents and accidents.

The only other lady teacher who I can remember by name was an elderly French lady called Mrs Going. She had snowy white hair and, with her frail look and excellent manners, was totally out of place. She was our music mistress and taught the piano, but not singing.

I have already mentioned our many headmasters. When we arrived, the headmaster was a Mr Wynne-Jones, who later went back to the UK to work as a reverend.[51] He had several children and I always felt that they got

---

51 He actually stayed in Tanganyika and became Bishop of Central Tanganyika.

preferential treatment. Mr Wynne-Jones was in such an elevated position vis-à-vis us non-English-speaking juniors that I have nothing really to say about him.

Our next headmaster was an ex-army major and an ex-teacher from Monkton Combe School here in England. His name was Major Lace and he has remained forever in my memory. He had two terrible character failings in my eyes. The first was that he never smiled except once a year on speech day and never, to my knowledge, laughed. The second was that he refused to acknowledge that half the pupils were girls and treated us all as boys. His regime was tough and he made the biggest changes in our daily routine.

He was followed by an Australian, Mr Doran, also an ex-missionary. The Dorans had four children, the youngest of whom, aged about two, had a hip problem and was, when he was with us, in a plaster cast with his legs splayed out. It must have been terrible in that heat.

The headmaster who was there when we left was Mr Langford-Smith, and I actually remember him as a person as by that time I was a prefect, a little tin god, and sat at the head table. He was English, married, with excellent manners, and quite unable to handle us.

Finally, two male teachers had a great influence on us. The first was English, a Mr Phillips. He too was ex-army and left us with a deep sigh of relief to take part in the victory parade in London after the Second World War. He was in early middle age, heavyset with a balding blond head. His temperament was terribly erratic, as was his behaviour, and I remember on one occasion he was invigilating the end-of-term exam when he took out a complete set of top and bottom dentures, put them on the desk and instructed us to go on working under their supervision while he went outside. As we had no idea for how long he would be gone, we went on working. On the other hand he was an excellent if strict teacher, and I always enjoyed his lessons, especially grammar.

I have left my favourite male teacher till last. He was an Australian, Gordon Chittleborough, aged in his late twenties, I would guess. He was tall, dark and handsome and an excellent athlete. Miss Wylie and Miss Newell both fancied him and made innumerable passes at him when we all, teachers and pupils, spent our little free time in the early evening on the playing field. He was a committed Christian, and continued his missionary work with us children. I always held that against him as I felt he was taking unfair advantage of his position, but on the other hand his integrity and honesty shone through whatever he did. He took us for lots of lessons and I particularly remember singing Schubert's *The Trout* under his direction.

He also took us for Swahili, which I never bothered with. It seemed a waste of time as I knew I wasn't going to spend the rest of my life there. Swahili is a made-up language, and the grammar is very difficult. However, it is very easy to read as it is pronounced exactly as written and I remember enthusiastically reading sections of the poem *Hiawatha* in Swahili. I did not understand a single word, but I liked the rhythm. I always got about 5% in my exams for answering each question with the Swahili version of 'I don't know.' As it was always my ambition to come top of the class, this meant that I had to work very hard and achieve very high marks in all my other subjects.

Prior to becoming a prefect I sat at Mr Chittleborough's table in the dining room and had many a battle, as he insisted that all plates were cleared and I often did not like the food. Stefan sat at Mrs Going's table and enjoyed much more food than he was entitled to as he ate everything that the others did not like.

Just as our teachers were a very mixed bunch, so were our fellow pupils. We had many nationalities – I can only recall a few – and each pupil had a tale to tell. We had Greeks (Anagnosteras, Fieros, Stradoudakis), Swiss (Ochsner), Russian/German (Muellers), Russian/American (Reusch), Italian (a young chap, very pleasant, whose name I cannot remember and who had a one-week journey to school from Zanzibar and died of some terrible disease while on holiday), English (Wynne-Jones), British but born in Africa (Francis), South African Boers (de Beer, van de Westhoven), Lebanese (Khouri), Swedish (Steudel), and of course the Austrians and Germans, already mentioned.

Because we could speak Greek we naturally gravitated towards that group, but once we had become fluent in English, we picked our friends because we liked them.

My special friend was called Cecil (named after Cecil Rhodes by her mother). She was and is (we are still in touch), a year older than I am, and to everyone except me, she is now known as Anne. We complemented each other very well. I helped her with her lessons and she, an accomplished and fearless athlete, encouraged me to play games with a modicum of enthusiasm. She had two sisters, and by sheer coincidence, when my cousin Franziska came to school, her best friend was Cecil's youngest sister, Bridget, always known as Chip. Although Cecil and I were never in the same class, we spent all our free time together and she helped to make my time at school happy.

I promised to give a taster of what our days were like. After breakfast, which consisted of porridge and two slices of bread spread very thinly with butter, we went back to change into our PT kit and did half an hour's PT – then back to shower and change into our school uniform, which for the girls was a gymslip in khaki (nothing else was available during the war) worn with a white blouse.

By nine we were in our classrooms. We had a fifteen-minute break mid-morning when we ate some fruit and got a drink of milk, then back to work until, I think, 12.30. A fairly quick lunch, which was always a cooked meal, then off to lie down for about forty-five minutes. This rest period was silent. Then back to work until four o'clock.

We got some more fruit and milk and now had a free three quarters of an hour, but unless we were ill, we were expected to make an appearance at the pool or at the tennis court. From five to six we had compulsory games. Then a shower and change, tea (which we very ready for), half an hour free, which we spent on the playing field, then an hour's homework and off to bed.

It was all very tightly controlled, but given the circumstances it was probably just as well. Major Lace added an extra bit of physical exertion to our day in that…

***

Sadly, this is where Lisa's account ends.

15

Repatriation

We knew that the war was drawing to a close and I was thrilled when Victory in Europe (VE) Day fell on my birthday in 1945.

During June 1946 we had a visit at our school from my father. Omama and Opapa were being repatriated to Cyprus before us, and as they could not speak English Dad was given fourteen days' leave to accompany them to Mombasa. Unfortunately he left his travel documents behind in Tabora, so when he arrived in Moshi he had to get special permission to enter Kenya. Back in Moshi on 8th June he came for a short visit before returning to Tabora.

We left school in the second term of 1946 as my parents wanted us home in case we too were to be repatriated soon. In fact it took about ten months, another lengthy period without any formal schooling. I suppose that my parents tried to continue with our education, but in a letter which I wrote to my friend Eva in March 1947 I say I am not doing any studying except for trying to relearn Greek with my dad.

Initially this wait in Tabora was enjoyable. The Italians were still there and so were most of the refugees. We visited friends, particularly Ulli, and played tennis, Monopoly and other games, but as time went on it got more boring as everyone seemed to be leaving.

By this time Uncle Hans and Aunt Edith lived in a house in Tabora near the railway station. I visited them frequently, usually cycling on my dad's bike with my leg through the crossbar. The distance was probably a little over a mile and so I went backward and forward several times a day. Attractions at my uncle's home included a radio, which had to be treated with great respect so as not to damage it. There were also home-made vanilla shortbread crescents dusted in icing sugar, and a confection of beaten egg white into which the yolk, also beaten with sugar, was stirred. I enjoyed my visits.

The Waldmanns in Tabora

On the way there were houses occupied by Indian railway employees. Lisa says that we knew some of them. I cannot remember them.

By 16th January 1947 the Italians had left, abandoning their cats and in some cases pet monkeys. Quite a few found sustenance and rest with us. We tried to keep them out of the house but it was not easy and some of the cats did gain access. One loved butter and if any was left on the table he was up there enjoying it. Another rather ugly cat loved my dad and used to spend long periods lying on his chest looking at him, or just sleeping.

We knew that we too would be leaving so tried not to give the cats too much to eat so that they would get used to foraging for themselves. After all, this was Africa and there should have been plenty of suitable wildlife for them. The monkeys did not make it into the house but they spent their time annoying the cats and trying to eat the food which we put outside.

Back in Tabora, I went to evensong at the Anglican church. As far as I can remember there was only one African Christian who came to that service. We became friends and used to walk home together until our paths for our respective homes diverged. He must have been older than me as I remember going to his house and meeting his wife, and he visited us at least once. There was still segregation in those days and I recall commenting to him that the fact that we could walk together was because we were both Christians and therefore one in Christ. Looked at in the light of present day, thinking this would be seen as very patronising, but it has to be recollected that I was only fourteen and living in very different times.

My father obviously expected to get back to sweet-making in Cyprus for he had ordered two hand-operated drop-roller machines from a company in Rochdale – William Brierley, Collier & Hartley Ltd. These had five sets of interchangeable rollers with different designs so that shaped sweets could be produced. They arrived in Africa in a black wooden crate, small but very heavy.

I was desperate to have a camera, and to my delight my parents somehow obtained a 35mm camera for me.

In April 1947 we finally left Tabora. The strays had to fend for themselves but our cook took our pet, Mausi. The cook and houseboy came to the station to see us off, waving as the train pulled out of the station. We were sorry to say goodbye, and I think that they were too.

We had been told we were going to be repatriated on a boat called *Orbita* and that may have been the reason why we initially travelled to Mombasa. Plans must have changed because we travelled down the Nile instead. This made our journey to Mombasa both unnecessary and illogical as we travelled there via Mwanza on Lake Victoria, the largest lake in Africa, out of which the White Nile flows. It did, however, mean that we had the chance to swim in the lake, in a corralled area to protect us from the crocodiles. In Mwanza my dad pointed out a cemetery, beautifully located overlooking the lake.

While in Mombasa we were housed in a refugee camp where most of the refugees were Polish. Accommodation was basic and consisted of long, dormitory-style huts, where individual families had partitioned off small areas with curtaining or other material to give some privacy. We queued up for food, which was provided on a communal basis. I did not enjoy the experience and it probably came as a bit of a culture shock to us, but it did not last long. Apart from the short while in Palestine in 1941, this was our only stay in a refugee camp throughout the war.

On one of our several train journeys in Kenya there had been an oil spillage on the line and the wheels of the train slipped. As a result the journey was quite jerky, and as the train was travelling over deep ravines, rather scary. There was some talk of sabotage.

From Mombasa we travelled to Nairobi. Here began our itinerary prepared by Thomas Cook for our journey down the Nile, involving not only steamers but also rail and motor transport. This was a wonderful experience.

The first stage from Nairobi, taking over twenty-seven hours, was by train to Namasagali. From there by steamer to Masindi Port, which lies on Lake Kyoga. Then to Butiaba by road on the shore of Lake Albert. From Butiaba we embarked on a boat and travelled on to Nimule, leaving there by car to Juba, which is in the Sudan.

On this part of the journey we met a photographer for an American picture magazine called *Life*. I was quite jealous of his photographic equipment. At one port of call we both went to a market and took photos, and I probably followed him around as surreptitiously as I could.

At one of the various trans-shipments we almost lost the little black crate containing our sweet-making machinery. The porters who were moving our things onto the boat tested it, and as it was so heavy, picked something lighter. My dad had to do some chasing about to get someone to put it aboard the steamer.

From Juba to Kosti we were on a Nile steamer for about seven days, travelling comfortably in first class and being well fed. I remember in the dining room two Roman Catholic priests, one of whom put a very large amount of salt on his food. They also only appeared to say grace at the end of the meal, which I thought was not right as we at Arusha had always said it 'fore and aft'.

On a small Nile steamer there is only a limited amount of things that one can do, and I suppose that once we got over the initial excitement the journey became rather boring. I remember sitting on the deck with Lisa and my dad, trying to relearn Greek. The Nile in this part of its course goes through huge reed beds and its true width is obscured by the vegetation. The boat would travel in a zig-zag fashion, bumping into the reed walls so as to push them back and so keep the channel open. I cannot remember my sleep being disturbed by the bumpiness, so I probably got used to it.

We disembarked at Kosti and travelled by rail to Khartoum, arriving in the early hours and finding it was already very hot. We were taken to the Grand Hotel, where we had a large room with a ceiling fan and a view over the gardens. Looking out over these, we saw that quite a number of the guests had had their beds taken out and were sleeping in the open air.

Khartoum, the capital of the Sudan, is situated at the confluence of the Blue and White Niles. It was in Khartoum that General Gordon was killed in a battle with the Mahdi who was a leader of a local force. The city was leafy with some impressive buildings. Adjoining it, and only separated by the Nile, is its twin city, called Omdurman. The contrast in those days between these two was incredible. We crossed a bridge from a green city and entered another where we saw just treeless desert. We wanted to go across because located there was the tomb of the Mahdi, which was impressive with its large, decorated dome. We also saw the house of the *Khalifa*, who had been an important local ruler.

From Khartoum by train to Wadi Halfa, the border town of Upper Egypt. There we embarked onto our last Nile steamer and travelled on to Shellal. Lisa and I had our fifteenth birthday on this boat. We were accompanied by two giraffes that were located at a lower level than us, and so we could stroke their heads.

The boat took us past Abu Simbel. This magnificent temple of Ancient Egypt was still in its original place at that time, but we did not pass close enough to it to get a good view. When the Aswan High Dam was built the temple was moved lock, stock and barrel to higher ground to preserve it as otherwise it would have been submerged in Lake Nasser. Years later, my wife Wendy and I were fortunate to have the chance to visit it at its new location when we were on holiday in Egypt.

From Shellal we entrained and travelled overnight to Cairo, arriving on 10th May. I assume we visited the Pyramids and Sphinx, and we were able to see the treasures of the tomb of Tutankhamen in the Cairo museum. A treat with my dad was being taken to Groppis, an ice cream parlour which he said was famous.

The final stage of our journey was from Port Said, where we embarked on the *Fouadieh*, the ferry which was to take us to Cyprus. This turned out to be the worst part of the trip because it was very rough and we were all seasick. I thought I was okay and sat down to a meal at a table with a New Zealand family, Mr and Mrs Clapham and their daughter Pauline. Mr Clapham advised me to eat something as this would help prevent seasickness, but it did not work.

We arrived in Cyprus on 14th May 1947.

16

Return to Cyprus 1947

On our return to Cyprus in May 1947, when I was fifteen, we initially moved into 2 Myron Street, Nicosia (which is now in the Turkish part of the city). We shared this one-storey house with my grandparents and a Greek widow with her two daughters, all three of whom lived in one room which had a separate entrance. As they had to bathe in their room, and as I slept in the hall with my bed next to the adjoining wall, I could sometimes hear them splashing about, which was probably embarrassing for the daughters.

Water for the house had to be pumped manually up to barrels on the roof from a well in the garden. We did this in the cool of the evening and the widow's daughters participated in this work. One of them took a fancy to me and we did a bit of smooching at the pump. It did not go on for long as my conscience got the better of me quite rapidly.

We did not have a fridge, and as it was very hot Omama used to go shopping to the market every morning. This was quite a trek, across the moat into the centre of the old city to the large market near to the Ayasofya mosque, as it was then known, which formerly had been a Christian church. Lisa or I accompanied her at times to help with the carrying. Omama no doubt haggled over the prices and I can recall her buying a piece of meat from the butcher to mince in front of her eyes. She then knew what was in the mince!

My parents had to arrange our schooling and find a suitable property where we could live as well as start to manufacture our sweets again. By

Stefan in Nicosia 1947

the end of May 1947 a lease for a one-storey house at 5 Norman Road had been signed, effective from 30th June. On 4th June I wrote to Eva and told her that I was going to attend the English School in Nicosia.

Our new home had six principal rooms. Initially I had a room to myself, but later moved into the lounge/dining room and slept on a chair which opened up into a rather narrow bed. I finally finished up with a room to myself once again.

The water supply was a bit different, having a reservoir in the garden which was replenished from a mains supply. The water still had to be pumped up to the tanks in the roof, but an electric pump did the job for us. As we were the last house on the mains, in the summer we often were short of water and had to buy expensively from vendors who came round with water carts.

The 'garden' was quite large but was simply a wilderness. There was a garage in which we installed the two drop-roller machines, and in there we manufactured toffees and hard-boiled sweets.

Omama and Opapa lived with us until 1950. Opapa had diabetes and was on insulin. Control of the condition in those days was difficult and complicated as urine had to be boiled with Erhlich or Benedict solution and then the colour change observed. I can remember him hurrying down the corridor, not very pleased if I got in his way when he was doing this. Omama was meticulous about ensuring that his meals were synchronised with the insulin. Nevertheless he had at least two hospital admissions with a diabetic coma.

Despite his age he had learned to read English, and in the afternoon he could be heard translating from the newspaper for Omama. He was a very good chess player but did not have much opposition and so used to amuse himself by playing against himself. He rarely played with me as I was nowhere near good enough to offer any competition.

Omama comes over in my memory as a warm and easy person and a very good cook. She thought nothing of spending the whole morning preparing a meal. We often nagged her to make Austrian specialities like potato dumplings filled with apricot, or even better, potato noodles covered with fried breadcrumbs, melted butter, sugar and perhaps cinnamon.

Despite their age, our grandparents wanted to return to Vienna to help run the Café Herrenhof. It came to nothing as on 26th August 1950, Omama died. Mutti must have known how ill she was as Uncle Hans came to Cyprus before she died. I knew she was ill as she had been in hospital, but I do not think I was fully aware of how serious it all was.

One evening I could hear her heavy, irregular breathing, and I went into another room to pray for her. As I prayed I could hear that the sound of that heavy breathing had ceased and I thought she was better, but in fact she had died. She was aged seventy-five.

I was eighteen but in those days still very much a minor, and I remember that I felt very pleased and important because I was able to accompany my dad and Uncle Hans while the necessary arrangements were made. Omama is buried near a village called Pyroi in a Jewish cemetery at Margo, which was donated by a Jewish farmer who had previously been settled there.

Opapa was devastated. He returned to Africa with his son and happily found Peggy, his youngest grandchild, a ray of sunshine in his declining years. He died on 16th March 1956 aged eighty-five and was buried in Dar es Salaam.

In September 1947 I started at the English School in Nicosia in Class 3. Most of the pupils were Greek. The school was situated on a slight hill perhaps two to three miles from our home, so I cycled there. I never had a bike stolen, though I once took someone else's by mistake from outside a shop and had to hurriedly ride back and return it, hopefully before the true owner turned up.

After a few weeks I was moved up to Class 4 (there were six classes altogether). Except for geometry I did reasonably well and at the end of the year I was fifth out of thirty-five boys. I had an advantage in that my English was better than a lot of the other students'. Sometimes, too, I could do some of my homework in class while things were being explained to the other boys.

Sport was not a shining success, though I did once make it into the first eleven for hockey. I was scared of the rather fierce sports master, so a highlight of my contact with him was when I hit him on the nose and made it bleed. He was trying to demonstrate the art of ducking to avoid a punch in boxing and he asked me to try to hit him on the nose. I was a bit reluctant, but he encouraged me to do so. When I connected with his nose I thought he would be angry, but in fairness to him he accepted that I had merely done what I had been told.

School can be a cruel place. One Armenian boy in particular was bullied terribly and must have had a miserable time. I did try to befriend him a little but think I could have done more.

At one time I started selling small bags of hard-boiled sweets to my schoolmates. It was reasonably popular for a while and I sometimes sold more than a pound's worth. This may not sound much now, but every little bit helped as we were short of money.

Shortly before term began in September 1948, we decided that I would not return to school so that I could help with the business. The plan was that my education up to matriculation would continue with the aid of a Wolsey Hall correspondence course. The cost of schooling, though not very high, may have been a factor too, but the main difference was another pair of hands at work.

Sometimes I tried learning Latin with my book propped up while boiling the sugar for the hard-boiled sweets. I also remember trying to study while sitting up with my dad at night when he was very ill with a heart attack in December 1950.

Anyway, I sat for my matriculation and passed four out of the five subjects. I even passed the maths paper, which included geometry. I failed Latin because I never mastered the grammar. Although my dad knew a lot of Latin it just did not seem to work to have him teach me. I got some private coaching and learned enough to get me a pass in January 1951. Although I had not 'matriculated', which required a pass in five subjects at one time, I was registered as a matriculated student of the University of London, which from a practical point of view was as good.

I would have liked to do medicine then, but it was impossible for me to get to medical school in England, firstly because we had no money, secondly because I was needed to work, and finally because I was not a Cypriot and not even naturalised British at that time, and so not eligible for a scholarship. Nevertheless, I still wanted to prepare for this plan and started going to evening classes in A Level chemistry. I found it very difficult and the course was discontinued because the University of London would not recognise the laboratory as adequate. Secretly, I was pleased.

As it seemed pretty obvious that medicine was out, my dad advised me to study something, and in view of his background law was the obvious choice. The University of London ran an external degree course in law and in 1954 I enrolled. My first examination was in 1954 and I passed the last one in 1956, so I managed to complete the course within the timescale of a full-time student. I read textbooks and some cribs such as *Nutshells* and *Questions and Answers* on the set subjects. That is not to say that I knew as much as full-time students, but I was able to answer the questions to the satisfaction of the examiner. I was, however, and still am, quite proud that I did the degree in those circumstances and in that timescale.

I regularly attended St. Paul's Anglican church, usually going to the 8am communion, 11am morning prayer and 6.30pm evensong. I also helped polish the brasses!

One day when I was fifteen or sixteen, a soldier who also attended St. Paul's invited me to go along with him to the Mission to Mediterranean Garrisons (MMG) after evensong. This was run by a couple of ladies. We spent most of the evening singing favourite hymns, usually the first and last verses. I really enjoyed it, but the first time I went was almost the last as I was out much later than normal. As I was walking home I met my parents looking for me, anxious and cross. They did not want me to go again, but we compromised and agreed that I would come home for ten o'clock, a rule that I stuck to for a long time.

Nicosia was a small place and at times I bumped into Mr Clapham, the New Zealander I had met on the *Fouadieh*. He invited me to go to a little meeting place called the Bethel Gospel Hall, situated in a courtyard in a side street in the Turkish quarter, but I did not accept his invitation. One evening he was the guest speaker at the MMG and after that I felt I could safely try it out. I initially continued at St. Paul's and at one time I was going to about six different meetings or services on a Sunday.

The congregation at the Bethel Gospel Hall were mainly Armenian, belonging to a Protestant group known as Brethren. The Brethren had strong doctrinal views and did not, for example, believe in a separate ordained ministry or a set liturgy. Their missionaries were not on regular salaries but preferred to live, as it was known, 'by faith', relying on God to provide for their needs through direct or indirect gifts from other believers. For doctrinal reasons the Brethren had very little if anything to do with other Christian denominations. This seemed terribly important to me at the time.

A missionary in his own right was an Armenian called Khatcher Kasparian. He was married to Melanie and had two children, Hilda and Jonathan. They lived by faith in a flat above the gospel hall, sometimes in straitened circumstances. I was a frequent visitor, as was a young second lieutenant, Peter Grosvenor, with whom I became good friends. One Christmas we shared a goose with Peter. This presented some problems because it had to be plucked. Also, I do not think we had a proper oven so I am not sure how we managed to cook it. It was common practice at that time for people to take their roasts to the baker, so perhaps we did that too. When Peter's first wife died he married Hilda Kasparian in 1997. We are still in touch and in fact until 10th January 2007 Melanie lived with them, and at times we went to 'granny-sit' to allow them to go away without concern. It also meant that we could have a lovely holiday, stay in their barn conversion, and visit several friends in the area.

The communion service at the Brethren is known as the breaking of bread, and is different to an Anglican communion. We used to sit in a circle. No one was in charge and any one of the men (not the ladies) could exercise a priestly function when he felt led by the Holy Spirit, and at times there were periods of silence. The service lasted about one and a half hours. Although it was open to all men to speak, in practice one or more of the missionaries took a more active part in leading the worship.

There were also weekday meetings, usually on Mondays and Wednesdays, but for a period Mr Clapham held special meetings on the tabernacle[52] and these were every night of the week. Most of the preaching was done in English and had to be translated, usually by Mr Kasparian and usually into Turkish as some of the older people were more fluent in this. Hymns were sung in different languages, but fortunately to the same tune. Prayers, as far as I remember, were not translated. One summer the services were taken by the Armenian Brethren but even though there was no translation into English I felt it my duty to support the meetings and spent the time reading religious books.

In the Christmas break we had extra services which we termed 'conferences', and at the New Year we had a watchnight service till midnight, so no excessive revelry. One Christmas we went carol-singing; not just Brethren families but also other Christians including an American minister who had arrived to head up a Pentecostal church. It was cold but clear and we were invited in by him for cake and excellent hot chocolate. It was just a lovely evening. We tried it again but it was never as good as that first time.

One evening when I was late for one of the midweek meetings I was either riding or scooting on my bike without lights. I was stopped and had to attend court, and was fined 4 shillings. My only court conviction arose because I was so keen to get to church!

As my involvement with the Brethren increased, my attendance at St. Paul's diminished and eventually ceased.

Mr Clapham was a very God-fearing man with strong Brethren views, and he was extremely keen on sharing the gospel with others. He knew the Bible well and could talk at length about it. I found it fascinating and at that time thought what he said to be vitally important. In 1955 I was asked to be on the organising committee for the Troodos conference, which was held under the auspices of the Reformed Presbyterians. It

---

52 See Exodus 25 onward.

was reported to me that Mr Clapham was not too happy about this and expressed the view that I was at a crossroads. Now that I think about it, he was probably right in his assessment of the effect it would have on my future relationships with other Christians. I shudder to think what he would now say about me!

My outstanding recollection of Mrs Clapham is that she thought that small quantities of kerosene (paraffin fuel) would help with various illnesses. Their daughter Pauline had long plaits and I found her attractive, but she was not interested in me. I was often invited to join the family for Sunday lunch. Mr Clapham played the piano well and I valiantly joined in the hymn-singing. I wonder what they thought of my efforts, as singing is not a strong point of mine! In the '50s the family returned to New Zealand where I understand Mrs Clapham lived to be over a hundred years old, cared for by Pauline, who never married.

I had Armenian friends including Arah Danielian and Hovsep (Joe) Pambakian. Both were slightly older than I, and very clever. After the Sunday afternoon meeting we often walked home together, engaging in long, spiritual discussions on the street corner where our paths diverged. They both left for England before me, where Arah became a physicist and Joe a pathologist. I am glad to have been able to retain their friendship.

Before Joe left in 1948 or 1949 he and I, together with others, were baptised in the sea near Kyrenia. The Brethren did not believe in infant baptism or sprinkling. Their view was that only believers should get baptised, and that it should be by total immersion.

Joe's brother Hamparzoum had a cloth shop where I spent many hours chatting with him between customers. In Cyprus buying material was not a simple matter. The purchaser would be told a price and be absolutely horrified at it. There would then be bargaining exchanges, with the customer sometimes threatening to leave. The trick was to be able to judge when the deal had to be struck, and Hamparzoum seemed to be good at this.

When he got engaged to Lucy, I sometimes went out with them to act as the required chaperone. One time we crossed some fields and walked into a small hut which turned out to be the Forces Broadcasting Studio. The surprised inhabitants said we were lucky not have been electrocuted, as the field we had crossed had contained various wires needed in connection with the broadcasts. Security was, perhaps, at that time not a top priority.

One of the older Armenian Brethren was a barber. Because of language barriers I could not converse with him. I felt it my duty to have my hair cut by him at least sometimes, but it was a bit of an ordeal as he used to pull my hair when using the manual clippers.

On one occasion, Melanie Kasparian's brother Edward got it into his head that we should all get up early on a Sunday and go out of doors to pray. We went along with this, but when he wanted to get up ever earlier the venture petered out.

Missionaries Jack Morris and his wife Gladys arrived from England intending to go on to Egypt once they got their visa. They needed somewhere to stay and my parents agreed that they could have a room in our house. (I think it was at this time that I moved into the lounge to sleep on the easy chair which opened up as a bed at night.) The Morrises never did get a visa and moved into their own home so that their two sons, Colin and Andrew, could join them from England. They were always hospitable and I made friends with the boys. Whilst in Cyprus, a daughter, Joy, was born to them.

At some point Minas Michaelides, who was Greek, joined us and became an active member. He and his Armenian wife Azniv were friends. In fact, looking back I must have been a real pain as I visited them frequently in the evenings after work. I remember when their daughter was born, the registrar misspelt her name. Minas was going to leave it but I thought the child would resent it when grown and I nagged them to get it corrected.

As we now had a Greek-speaker it was decided to try to have open-air meetings in the Greek-speaking part of the town. Someone made large banners, one of which I remember was a picture of the broad and narrow ways leading respectively to Hell and Heaven. We usually held the meetings in Metaxas Square on the ramparts in the Greek section. Those who were not engaged in holding the banner or preaching used to stand around handing out leaflets, many of which we got from the Scripture Gift Mission. Most people took them quite readily but I do not recall a single Greek Orthodox person coming to our meeting as a result. We went out once and sometimes twice a week for quite a long time. For a while we also went to Larnaca, travelling in a van owned by Joe's uncle who had a soft drink factory. It was great fun as we were all young together.

After a time I was informed that under the Missionary Educational and Medical (Aliens Regulations) Law, I had to apply for a licence to undertake this work. After giving an undertaking, permission was granted and published in the *Gazette* dated 31st January 1953. I had always wanted to do some missionary work, and although I do not think this was the real thing it is in black and white that I was registered as a missionary.

At some point the Palmers, another New Zealand missionary family with four children, arrived. They settled in Larnaca, intending to start up a meeting there. I liked them and quite frequently went to Larnaca and spent Sunday with them. Although I would not have admitted it, I suspect that Lois, their eldest daughter who was very attractive, was part of the draw.

There were still Jewish refugees who had been stopped from entering Palestine housed in camps in Cyprus, and Mr Palmer was keen to go and preach to them. As a lot of the people spoke German I, with my limited German, acted as his interpreter. After one of the meetings we were invited to go for a drink. I had a soft drink and our host invited Mr Palmer to join him in an alcoholic drink. I knew Mr Palmer disapproved of alcohol and was shocked when, after initially demurring, he accepted. He later explained to me that he had felt that it was the right thing to do in the circumstances. Nevertheless it left a lasting impression on me and perhaps was one of the influences which gradually undid some of the rigid certainties I had learned from these New Zealand missionaries.

One summer I was invited to join the Palmers when they were camping in the Troodos mountains near Prodromos. While there Mr Palmer decided that he was going to make a man of me and asked me to help kill a chicken which we would then eat. All I had to do was to hold the bird while he did the deed. All went well for a few moments, but I then let go and it sprayed blood all over the place. I was never asked to help again.

The family finally returned to New Zealand and I never had any further contact with them.

The small group of Christians who had come together for Sunday meetings in Larnaca were now on their own, and so for some time I used to go and take the services for them. As I insisted on staying for the breaking of bread service in Nicosia it was about 11am and hot before I left. I used to cycle the twenty-six miles to Larnaca over undulating roads. It took me about two hours as I only had an old, heavy bike with three gears, if any at all. The first time I went the wind was behind me and I did it in record time. However, when I cycled home that evening the wind was against me and as Nicosia is above sea level the route was more uphill than down. It took me four or five hours to get back and I was completely exhausted. After that I always did the return journey on the bus, which fortunately could take bicycles.

An Armenian family named Sarafian held the Larnaca meetings at their home and I was often given lunch by them when I arrived, but sometimes it was a Greek lady whose surname was Trompettas who fed me. I cannot now remember when these meetings came to an end.

Meanwhile my twin sister was having different experiences. She enrolled at the American Academy in Nicosia, but tired of it and left. She taught herself typing on the Olivetti portable typewriter and Gregg shorthand, in which she became very proficient.

Lisa says that she got up early to clean the house (needless to say, I don't remember anything about this), and she also helped with the sweets. The hard-boiled sweets had to be wrapped by hand, a skilled task as it had to be done quickly but the twists had to be tight. I was very slow in contrast to Lisa and Mutti, who could do it quickly and well.

Having left school, Lisa wanted to work to earn money. Showing considerable initiative, she went to see the American Consul in his hotel and persuaded him to give her a job despite her inexperience. She retained this till she left Cyprus after her wedding.

She loved to go to dances, chaperoned by Mutti, where she met servicemen stationed in Nicosia. We got to know George, a Geordie who used to visit us in the evenings. We used to sit round a smelly paraffin stove as it could be cold in winter. The evenings must have been exciting because we all fell asleep until it was time for George to go home!

Lisa met and got engaged to Shane Whitehouse, who was in the RAF, very handsome and the son of a clergyman. He was a good cyclist and I was filled with admiration when I learned that he had cycled up to Troodos as well as down. That is quite an achievement as Troodos is about 6,000 feet (1,850 metres) above sea level.

Lisa and Shane were married by Rev. Adeney at St. Paul's in Nicosia on 4th September 1950. They went to Platres, a mountain resort, for their honeymoon. From there, even though they were only a few miles away from us and only gone for a few days, Lisa wrote letters to Mutti. In January 1951 they left for England, returning in 1956.

17

Sweet Making

The family sweet-making business was vitally important to us.

Initially we concentrated on boiled sweets using our drop-roller machines. Sugar was boiled in large, lined copper kettles over very large Primus stoves. A Primus stove burns paraffin under pressure and is very noisy.

Once the sugar solution reached the correct temperature it was poured – a potentially dangerous activity – onto thick stone slabs. Ideally these should have been marble but we could not afford that, so used a cement slab with embedded fragments of marble or stone. This had a tendency to crumble and we had to try to make sure that cement or stones were taken out of the sugar before it went through the drop-roller machines. Presumably we were successful, as I know of no complaint.

In addition to hard-boiled sweets and toffees we also made fondant creams and jellies. All the wrapping and packing was done in the house.

Making sweets the way we did was labour-intensive. Initially we did not have help with the manufacturing process as we could not afford it, and there were two of us anyway. We did, however, need help with the wrapping, packing and washing as, especially once Lisa left, Mutti would have been on her own. Most of the girls we employed to help were Greek.

When I first started helping, Dad did all the dangerous activities and insisted on turning the drop-roller machines. This was hard work and often he had to sit down afterwards because he had pain. No doubt this was associated with angina, though I did not realise it at the time. As time progressed I was able to do the hard work. Making sweets with my dad was not all drudgery though, for he knew many German songs and we used to sing as we worked.

At one time we had thoughts of making chocolate-coated wares, but it came to nothing. While on the subject of chocolate, I can remember that one of our customers imported Easter eggs, many of which were smashed, and my father bought some of these, I imagine at knock-down prices. As we could not turn the broken chocolate into money, we enjoyed eating it!

To get the orders in Nicosia we walked round the wholesalers and a few retail outlets. Before he became too ill, Dad and I often walked to town together, stopping to rest at a typical Greek café situated at the Paphos Gate, very near the Roman Catholic church. We sat on straight-backed chairs with woven seats, drinking little cups of coffee served with ice-cold water. Another chair was used as a table, and up to four more to rest one's arms and legs. It was common practice so presumably the coffee shop had an ample number of chairs.

Having rested, we continued to try to get orders. One of the first shops we came to was owned by an Armenian sweet manufacturer who, among other things, also roasted nuts and seeds. These were displayed in large sacks and while my dad did the business I used to help myself to a snack from them, openly but not too obviously as I feared that the owners would not have approved! I would probably disapprove of such conduct now, but times were different then.

In the afternoon we delivered orders. We had no car initially and if I could not make the delivery on my bicycle we had to get a taxi. After the drops were completed I sometimes accompanied my parents to Metaxas Square where they socialised with other refugees in a coffee shop run by a lady of either Austrian or German descent.

While he was able my dad also used to go to other towns, presumably by public transport, to sell our products. Paphos, though only about one hundred miles away, required an overnight stay. I recall how pleased my dad was when on one occasion upon his return he told us that one of his customers had paid him an outstanding bill from before we were evacuated in the early 1940s.

Because it was only just after the war, sugar was rationed. This had, I think, at least one advantage as it limited supply and therefore price competition from several other sweet manufacturers who were better placed financially than we were. As sugar became more readily available these manufacturers were able to undercut us, sometimes selling hard-boiled sweets at or below our cost price. As we never put in any cost for our personal wages, our income was restricted to the mark-up only.

To survive we had to find innovative packaging and products. None of our competitors made jellies, but there was only a very limited market. We tried fondant sugar mice, but these were soon copied. Novel ways of packaging worked for a time until also copied. We had to try to find products which would not be copied, or customers who were not reached by our competitors.

Although the competition was fierce, the competitors were not necessarily unfriendly. For instance, if it had not been for Mr Dascalopoulos, who sold us small quantities of items which we needed but could not afford to buy in bulk, we may not have survived. I cycled with a big tin container over to his home to buy glucose from him. This came in big drums, but it was seldom that we could buy one of these. Once the tin was filled it might have contained fifty kilos. I strapped it on the carrier of the bike and cycled gingerly home.

For a while Dad managed to sell to the Jewish refugee camps through another Austrian refugee, Mr Tauber. One day, however, he told my dad that he could not buy any more of our products because his customers had heard that I was a Christian and they did not want anything to do with us. Maybe someone had found out that I used to go to the camps with Mr Palmer. Losing their business was, of course, a blow. It was also the only occasion that I am aware of that we were discriminated against because of my religious belief.

Nobody was manufacturing wafers in Cyprus, but my dad knew that these had been popular in Vienna. However, the only English machines he could locate were huge and very expensive, and even the relatively small ones from Vienna were beyond his means.

I think from a casual conversation with a German person Dad heard about the International Hebrew Christian Alliance. With a supporting letter from Mr Clapham to Rev. Harcourt Samuel, the executive secretary, my father asked for their financial help. On 8th April 1949 they agreed to lend us £450 interest-free. The intention was that we should pay off the loan at £50 every six months, but in fact we failed miserably in this.

After various complications regarding import and export licences we ordered the machinery and in mid-November 1949 two electrically heated wafer tongs, producing wafers sized twenty-seven by thirty-seven centimetres, arrived. One of them was engraved with small squares or diagonals and the other had an oval design with the word *REX*. We also bought a manual filling machine and a cutting table with its accessories.

A 'pancake' mix was used to make the wafers. Once the machines were heated to the right temperature, the baking began. When we first tried them out we had not realised that there were vent holes at the corners, out of which shot steam and surplus mix. We had pancake mix all round the room, and it was also quite noisy. We learned from experience and got metal corners made, which we put around the machines so that the blowout could be contained and later disposed of. Wafers are very hydroscopic and so we had to find ways of keeping them as flat as possible, otherwise filling them with chocolate or another flavoured filling was very difficult indeed. I usually did the filling.

The cutting table was potentially dangerous as it had several circular saw blades driven by an electric motor. The unguarded saws protruded above the working surface and the large rectangular wafers had to be pushed through the blades. There was always a moment when the wafer had passed through that one's hand and arms were right over the blades. Despite this, in all the years we used this cutting table, no one hurt themselves.

This was all new to us, which probably explains why my dad had not realised that we could not sell the wafers in the hot season as the fillings melted. He also found that the market was more limited than he had expected – a big disappointment for us.

In December 1950 my father had his first heart attack. He had already been suffering with angina, but one afternoon after lunch he fell ill with chest pain and had to go to bed. Dr Pietroni, who was our doctor, said he had to stay in bed for twenty-one days. Initially at least he was not supposed to even move his hand to scratch his nose. We took it in turns to sit up with him, day and night. There must have been a further event, for I recall Dr Pietroni coming to the house in the night and looking very grave after he had examined Dad. My father survived, but he was unable to do heavy work.

Despite the fact that sales were not what we had hoped for, and my dad's heart attack, in 1951 the Hebrew Christians loaned us another £400.

My dad wrote and said he was working in partnership with me, and that I would be a co-signer of the debt and therefore under personal obligation. In addition, he would hand over the property in the machinery to them. As far as I know, no formal partnership arrangements were entered into until March 1956. Whether I was aware of the letter when it was written I cannot now say, though I suspect I was. However, I had always expected to be responsible for the debt, for as far as I was concerned we were in it together.

Over the years we had made a few small repayments, but the first time we actually managed to send the full sum of £50 was not until January 1956, and we were by then well behind in our repayments. My father died on 23rd August and by the time I left Cyprus in 1957 we had repaid £310, leaving a balance of £540.

Following my arrival in England in the late '50s I went to see Rev. Harcourt Samuel in London. I formed the impression that there was no hurry to repay the balance. I remember leaving the offices and walking along with a light tread as I felt so relieved, for I had only just enough to establish myself in England. There then followed a long hiatus, and prompted by Wendy, my wife whom I married in 1961, I restarted repayment in 1966 and finally got the loan repaid in 1975. Out of gratitude, I continued with a small gift by standing order for about another twenty-four years.

It was only when I came to cancel the standing order in 1999 that I realised that the Hebrew Christians should have had the wafer machinery which I had sold when I left Cyprus, or at the least I should have handed the proceeds over there and then. I wrote to them and said I was very sorry about this, and they replied in their usual generous way, saying I was not to worry about it.

I cannot emphasise enough how fundamentally important the help and forbearance from the Hebrew Christians was to our survival, and I have always remained extremely grateful to them for what they did for us and for the God-honouring way they behaved throughout. Thank you again.

Wafer wrapper.

Things must have looked pretty grim business-wise. We were unable to effectively compete on conventional hard-boiled sweets. Our wafers, on which we had set such store, only had a limited season and even then did not sell in the quantities we had hoped for, and on top of this my dad was now gravely ill. Our financial position remained precarious.

Dad could still do non-physical work and, most importantly, come up with ideas. He also spoke German, so could access literature in that language. In a German catering magazine he read about moulds for sugar whistles that really whistled. Needless to say there were some huge machines available in England which also made these, but these were of no interest to us. We ordered perhaps ten to fifteen moulds. Of course we had never seen them before and we had no idea how difficult it was to use them.

It took weeks of practice. The moulds had to be held at a correct angle to coat the inside with sugar, yet produce a hollow object of the right shape. They also became very hot, but to keep the process going we had to go on reusing them, which meant it became more and more difficult to get the whistles out of the moulds.

It was also easy to get one's finger burned, but I soon learned, along with Colin Morris[53] who worked with us for us for a time, that cold water was effective in these cases, and as far as I know we never suffered any significant burns. Colin and I were helped by a Greek girl called Maria, who was quite small but an exceptionally efficient worker.

We were never copied but with a small population there were only so many whistles we could sell, and I suppose too that there were limits on the quantities we could actually produce. It was indeed very hot work as we made whistles in the summer months when the temperature could rise to forty degrees Celsius and sometimes even higher. This was compounded by the Primus stoves, which we needed to boil the sugar.

After my dad became ill I started making the deliveries. In Nicosia I could sometimes do this using my bike, but if we needed a taxi my parents would be able to come along. Public transport was needed to get to other locations. Sometimes I took my bike on the bus to help make deliveries at the destination.

---

53 Colin was the older son of the missionary couple, Jack and Gladys, who had stayed with us for some time.

Most of our output was sold to wholesalers in towns. Selling direct to retail outlets has the advantage that one can avoid the wholesale discount, but to reach the villages would require a car. This was the justification for asking the Hebrew Christians for the further loan of £400 previously mentioned, and which we received around the end of 1951.

All the vehicles we had in Cyprus were second-hand. Our first car had the same registration as our telephone number: 2895. It should have been a good omen, but it did not live up to it. In a letter to the Hebrew Christians my dad described one of our vehicles as a good car, but that, I think, was a terminological inexactitude as in fact our cars spent a lot of time in the garage being repaired. The dynamo had frequently to be repaired by an auto electrician with replacement brushes or rewinding of the armature. I spent a fair bit of time sitting around in garages!

We had got a phone because it obviously was useful for business, but mainly in case my father needed a doctor urgently again, for when Dr Pietroni had come to see him during the night (as mentioned earlier) I had had to go, probably on my bike, to fetch him from his home.

After we got the car for a short time we employed a Greek Cypriot to help us try to expand into villages and smaller townships, but that did not work and he left us. I only remember a long journey with him up 'the panhandle of Cyprus'. We stayed overnight in St. Andrea's Monastery at the tip, where I think accommodation and a meal of bread and cheese was free.

The car did make visits to the towns easier, and I could collect the orders and make the drops in one. If I had to stay overnight in Paphos I used to bed down in the New Olympus Hotel.

I do recall a nightmare journey when I intended to do a round trip to Paphos via Polis and perhaps other places, returning by way of Limassol. Everything went reasonably well until I got near to the town of Polis. The shaft on the dynamo broke and so I had no power or fan belt, but somehow I got to Polis. The auto electrician said the dynamo was beyond repair and there was no replacement part. I must have kicked up a fuss because someone with a lathe decided to try to turn another shaft. The dynamo was repaired and repositioned and after a long delay I set off towards Paphos. However, the electrician was right because not many miles down the road it broke again. Luckily most of the road was downhill and so I was able to limp into Paphos by coasting down. The car then had to be repaired again, and next morning I set off towards Limassol.

A short distance from Paphos something again went wrong, so I opened the bonnet to investigate. The car could be started by pressing a button under the bonnet to activate the starter motor. I did this but forgot about my other hand, and one of my fingers was caught by the fan belt and trapped in the upper pulley attached to the dynamo. It was fortunate that the engine did not start. I called for help to a local resident who was passing by on a bike, but he said that he did not know anything about cars! It was just as well for him that I was tethered! Shortly after that someone stopped and released the belt tension and I was able to get my finger out. I presumably thanked him, then returned to Paphos, this time to the local hospital and perhaps also to get the car looked at again. My finger was dressed and I went on my way. I did not get home till very late, so there may have been other problems too. I hope I did sell something as I would have needed the money to pay for all the repairs!

Having the car meant I could stop for a rest or lunch and look round at the many ancient monuments along the way, for example Curium with its lovely amphitheatre overlooking the sea. In the evenings and weekends the car also provided mobility for my parents and me.

On some of my selling trips I would take someone with me for the ride and a day out. I remember taking Colin and enjoying a lovely watermelon for lunch, picnicking in a field.

Sometimes Mr Kasparian would accompany me. He had obtained a gramophone from an evangelical organisation in England, with Greek-language records of gospel talks. At times he used to take this with him, and while I was trying to sell he set it up and played the records to the local population. Both of us would have been pleased to have this opportunity of sharing the gospel.

Other towns visited including Kyrenia, but it did not have many customers for our goods. In Larnaca we had an important customer, Mr Nicolaides, who had a shop very near the centre of the town. As was customary in Cyprus, I would have been treated to a small cup of strong coffee with plenty of ice-cold water.

Famagusta was a much bigger place than Larnaca and we had several customers, but the only one I remember was only able to make minimal purchases. This was a Christian outreach centre not dissimilar to the

MMG, which was run by Dr Shelley, a devout conservative evangelical Christian associated with the Brethren. As I understood it, he had gone to settle in Jerusalem because he wanted to be there when the Lord Jesus returned. I assume that he left when the state of Israel was founded, and he and other relatives settled in Cyprus. One of these had a dental practice in Nicosia but it was far too expensive for me to go to him.

Perhaps because I went to the Bethel Gospel Hall, Dr Shelley usually invited me to stay for lunch, which was quite a formal affair where the various courses were served by his housekeeper. When we finished a course Dr Shelley used to ring a bell and the housekeeper cleared the table and served the next course. From a business point of view the visits were not significant, but I enjoyed his company as well as the food.

During this time we were mostly on the breadline. We were lucky with our landlord for we often could not pay the rent on time, but we somehow muddled through.

At some time during this period we got a customer not open to our competitors, who was located on the RAF station. It was a charity known as Hibbert House, which operated a canteen and shop and also had a sandwich round on the RAF station. They were good customers, and I got to know the people running it quite well.

At one time they were short of a driver to do the morning round, and I volunteered. I had a pass to enter the RAF station which enabled me to get onto the site, but I doubt it was intended to cover me driving all round the station. I had no problems, though.

Financially, however, things did not start to look up until 1955 when we eventually managed to persuade the NAAFI[54] to buy our products. We had tried before and failed, but now, having wafers to offer, we succeeded. In the cooler weather we found a ready market for our large-sized wafers, which were wrapped in silver foil with a paper band printed with the word REX.

We had at last found a large, exclusive customer and were able to sell direct without a middleman, so were able to command a good price for the product. The NAAFI had canteens situated in most camps or barracks, and because of the EOKA[55] insurgency troop numbers

---

54   The organisation that supplies recreational facilities, runs canteens and provides goods for sale to armed forces personnel and their families.

55   National Organisation of Cypriot fighters (a Greek Cypriot nationalist organisation).

increased, which of course was good for business. I had a pass and so could enter the camps.

In addition to the invoiced boxes I used to leave a number of the wafer biscuits with the manager or deputy as a gift. The intention, no doubt, was to encourage them to display our product prominently so that the servicemen would buy them. I now feel a bit guilty about this, but survival, I suppose, was the name of the game.

There were, however, clouds in the sky. Firstly, we had become entirely dependent on one customer – always an unsafe position. More importantly, the quality of our product slipped because additional second-hand machines, which we had bought from Germany, did not work so well.

But having said this, the period from perhaps autumn 1955 till I left at the end of 1957 was the best and most profitable period that we had enjoyed since 1947.

18

Daily Life in Cyprus

Lunch was the main meal of the day and the table was properly laid. While Lisa was still with us I liked the symmetry of sitting at a square table, balanced numerically by gender and also because Lisa and I were twins.

We often ate beef broth followed by the meat which had been cooked in it, with sauté potatoes as for a long time we had no oven. Fruit was plentiful and cheap. Mutti particularly liked one variety of large grapes called Verigo.

In the evenings when it was cooler we used to sit on the veranda, and ate whatever was available. Bread and homemade pork dripping, or bread dipped in sweetened yogurt, was cheap and I enjoyed it.

The yogurt, made from sheep's or goats' milk, was delicious. At one time a man with a cart used to come round, calling out, "*Gala Oxino*", which in Greek means 'sour milk'. We bought yogurt from him, which was set in different-sized earthenware containers. It had a thick skin on it which was not always clean, but that did not seem to worry me much. The empty containers were returned to the vendor.

I occasionally bought a kebab (*souflakia*) from one of the numerous vendors dotted about the place. Cyprus kebabs, in my opinion, are very much superior to those we can get in England. They were not that expensive but still a luxury for me.

Nicosia also had many patisseries making Greek or Turkish-style cakes, and in some cases ice cream. Some of the owners were customers and I enjoyed buying a cake when I was in town doing business. Sometimes I treated myself to a delicious cake or cheese pastry from a more upmarket patisserie called the Hurricane, opened by a Greek from Egypt. In contrast there was a small Armenian trader in a rather run-down and dingy location. He made *Lokmades*, which are little yeast dough balls, deep-fried and then drenched in syrup. I loved these and still do.

Because of the tremendous heat in the summer, cold drinks and ice cream were almost a must. Initially, as many households and indeed traders did not have fridges or freezers, blocks of ice had to be purchased to cool the drinks. Until we got a fridge we just had a small, insulated icebox, and in the summer we daily bought part of an ice block to keep food fresh and to have some cold water. An alternative way of cooling water was to place it in non-glazed earthenware containers. These allowed moisture to leak through, and this evaporated and cooled the contents. It was cheap but not as good as ice.

Ice cream was home-made by the vendors, but as shops acquired freezers, Lyons' and Wall's ice cream penetrated the market. Perhaps on a Sunday I might ride or drive over to Metaxas Square to one of the kiosks and buy a block of English ice cream to take home.

We did not particularly like the standard Cypriot round loaves of bread. We enjoyed a white bread covered in sesame seeds called *guluri* but it was too expensive to eat regularly. A continental-style bakery opened sometime in the '50s and became very popular with us and others.

There were virtually no cows in Cyprus and so we used unsweetened condensed milk. Hard local cheeses like *kefalotiri* or *kaskavali* were very expensive, and the more reasonably priced halloumi we despised and thought too hard and salty. We mainly bought imported cheese like Edam or Gouda.

One thing we had plenty of was cockroaches, which must have come up from the drains. We had to wash them down before we could use the sink, which was made of stone. We did not like the little creatures but one learns to live with them.

My parents were not churchgoers so found their social contacts elsewhere. Fortunately there were several German-speaking Jewish families living in Nicosia. One of these was the Zimbler family, whose daughter Lisa's bike I had envied when we were at school in Larnaca. Nothing changed as she now drove a Rover, which I also coveted. Compared to us the family were quite well off. In contrast the

Fleishmanns, whom we also spent time with, were probably in the same straits as us. The wife was a dressmaker but I never found out exactly what the husband did.

Mrs Tauber, the widow of the man who had stopped buying our products for the refugee camps, was another contact. She played bridge at home, and I wanted to learn to play. I enjoyed the game but she insisted that one had to play for money to make the bidding realistic. Only pennies were involved, but it seemed to me to be gambling and my conscience at that time made me stop going.

One day my parents arranged for us to visit another Jewish family. I now think the reason was that they had a daughter and our respective parents wanted us to meet. As far as I was concerned it was a lost cause, for I did not think she was a Christian. Oddly enough, in a very old Bible of mine I found an address in London for someone who may have been this daughter. I do not remember ever calling on her, so do not know why I noted the address.

There were at least two other matchmaking possibilities that arose. In a letter Mutti wrote, it seems that in 1954 there was a proposal for a match with a dentist's daughter. She had a good dowry but it seems that neither Mutti nor I were interested. If it were not for the letter I would have no recollection of this at all.

In 1956 someone I knew in Nicosia told me that he would be willing to arrange a match with a Christian girl who at that time was living in Athens. This girl did write me a letter, and when I was passing through Athens on one occasion I visited the family but nothing came of it. I know that she has married and has children and hope that she has had a very happy life.

There were lots of open-air coffee shops which did a roaring trade on summer evenings. One could order a soft drink, coffee or alcoholic beverages like ouzo or brandy, which were very cheap in Cyprus. The alcoholic drinks came with meze, numerous tiny plates with small quantities of nibbles such as olives, nuts and tahini.

Someone took the plunge and built the splendid Ledra Palace Hotel, modelled on the Doge's Palace in Venice. My parents discovered that on a summer's evening they could have a drink, sit in the lovely garden, and listen to music and watch the dancing. It was smart and attractive and they enjoyed being there. I used to pick them up and stay for a while, enjoying the venue.

Sometimes my parents went to the open-air cinemas. At that time I disapproved of cinemas as being worldly, and so generally would not go. I remember my dad being quite upset because I would not go with them to see *Quo Vadis*. After he died I did go and see it, to make up I suppose. I did, however, see *The Song of Bernadette* with Vivien Leigh as the lead. This is a story about a girl in France who had a vision of a lady, presumed to be the Virgin Mary. The story was written by Franz Werfel, a Jewish refugee from Vienna who had initially fled to France. When the Nazis captured France he apparently said that he would write the story as a thank-you if he escaped. I was very moved by this film, though I could not accept the Roman Catholic doctrine of the Immaculate Conception.

Sometime in the early '50s my father found out that by signing the visitors' book at the Governor's House we would in due course receive an invitation to attend official receptions for events like the Queen's birthday. So we went along and mingled with the great and the good. I think that there I met one of the assistant commissioners, which probably proved useful during the EOKA emergency.

One of the highlights of my life was going to the American Academy campsite high up in the Troodos mountains, where each year for the first few days of August there was a Christian summer camp. We sang metrical psalms, had Bible studies, sat round a campfire, walked up to Troodos, washed dishes and peeled spuds, played games and generally enjoyed ourselves, recovering from the heat of the plain. Many of the Christians were not associated with the Brethren, so my circle of friends enlarged.

We travelled up to the camp by bus. On the way up we passed a village called Amiandos. This is the Greek word for 'asbestos', and there was an opencast mine for this material with clouds of dust everywhere. I now shudder to think what it did to the lungs of those who worked there.

In Nicosia in those days the working week was five and a half days, so we had Saturday afternoon off. In the summer we often used to cross the Kyrenia mountain range to go to the sea to swim. At times we took our bikes on the bus and then at the top of the pass got off and rode down to Kyrenia. It was an exhilarating sensation going at speed downhill with the wind blowing in my face. After the swim on the way back we sometimes stopped at Newman's Farm on the outskirts of Kyrenia. This farm had cows, a rarity in Cyprus in those days, and they sold cold milk to drink.

The year 1950 must have been an extra-hard time for my parents –

particularly for Mutti. As well as the continuing financial problems, Omama had died on 26th August, and Lisa got married on 4th September and left Cyprus to settle in England in the beginning of 1951. My dad had a coronary thrombosis in December 1950, and Opapa left for Africa around this time too. Within the space of a few months, Mutti, for practical purposes, lost both her parents, her only daughter, and was left with an invalid husband. Hard as it must have been, I cannot remember her complaining or not getting on with life.

In the 1950's it had become possible to apply for British nationality. My parents had no intention to resettle in Austria, and as I felt much more British than Austrian it made sense that we should get our status sorted out.

My dad was granted citizenship in 1953, but I was just too old to come in under his application and so had to apply in my own right. My application was granted on 12th July 1954. I applied for a passport and was issued with one that indicated that I was a British citizen of Cyprus. I wanted to be considered a British citizen of the UK, so I reapplied for a passport to be issued in England and in due course this was sent from Peterborough. This proved a very astute move because it meant that when the EOKA insurgency started, my passport status was similar to that of expatriate UK citizens.

Cyprus was a Crown Colony, but the Greek-speaking majority on the island wanted enosis, or union with Greece. This was strongly opposed by the Turkish minority and the British. The Greek Orthodox church under Archbishop Makarios III was in the forefront of the political struggle, with Greek flags flying from churches. An organisation was set up known as EOKA, led by Colonel Grivas, and on 1st April 1955 a bombing campaign began.

The conflict polarised the population, with the Turks siding with the British. Of course my sympathies lay with the British. I considered myself an expatriate and, although at that time I had never been to England, identified myself as English. I also had a lot of military friends.

I had to go into town because of my business, and in any case I did not feel that I should be scared of going out. Cars had to be immobilised in town and I used to remove part of the distributor so that it was not possible to start the vehicle.

I tried to be careful and tended to look around to see if I was being followed. I was once told by a friend who had a shop in Ledra Street that people had been in to ask who I was, but I was never threatened or involved in any disturbance. One time though, I was near a very large church near the centre of Nicosia called Phanaromeni when a procession started. I was ahead of it and decided to turn in one direction, and the procession turned the other way. I think I did well as I believe two people got shot on that occasion.

The EOKA emergency led to various restrictions including frequent curfews, but often these did not apply to me as I had managed to get a curfew pass and often ferried heavily armed troops to and from some meeting or another.

I was definitely out and about in March 1956 on the night that Archbishop Makarios was arrested. I was driving my car, which was full of heavily armed servicemen who I was returning to their base. We were stopped by a patrol and I think asked if we had any arms. When we said clearly that we had, they pointed a gun at my head and ordered us out of the vehicle. We were able to satisfy them of our status and then went on our way.

I had a very negative attitude towards the Greek Orthodox church, which was very different to the evangelical Christianity I was used to, so I can remember how thrilled I was when I discovered an Orthodox bookshop in Larnaca called Anagenesis (Born Again) – a very evangelical-sounding name!

I think it likely that we had to stop holding our open-air meetings in the Greek sector. We had never had an effective open-air witness in the Turkish sector, but I have a feeling that at some point we did have one or perhaps two attempts. It was (and no doubt still is) very difficult to evangelise in a Muslim society. I only knew one ex-Muslim Christian in Cyprus, and he went to the Academy church.

With time Christians with less rigid views came to the island and my contacts broadened. Among these were Bill and Olive Cross and their family. They settled in Limassol. I visited regularly and was always made very welcome. Bill was setting up a cement plant near Limassol and by my standards was wealthy. There were other Christians in Limassol too, including an army doctor, Dr Kendal, and his family. It was while I was staying with them in London on my first visit to England in August 1956 that I learned that my dad had died.

Particularly after the EOKA uprising, when the inner city became out of bounds to service personnel, we used to meet at the Morrises' home on a Sunday evening for something to eat and for a Bible study or something similar. We also had a Bible study evening during the week in our home, which was attended by service personnel and a few others. Service personnel were only allowed out if armed, and our homes bristled with Sten and Bren guns on Bible study nights. My parents gave up the lounge for our use.

An American missionary named Hilda Miles came along, as did two Greek girls, Maroulla and Tilda. I do not think I thought about it at the time, but on reflection they may have been taking considerable risks by openly associating with servicemen.

I liked Tilda and can still remember the trepidation I felt when I first asked her to go out with me. Occasionally we bought delicious Cyprus kebabs and ate them sitting in the car. Our friendship remained purely platonic.

Tilda's brother Hercules worked for Cyprus Airways and I often visited him and his wife Nouvart at their home. When Tilda was there, that was a bonus. In due course she settled in England and is married to Alan Viller, a clergyman. At the time of writing we are still in contact.

In 1954, military nurses arrived in Nicosia. I started going out with one of them, which would have been frowned on as we were not married. I did not want to subscribe to this view but did have very strict ideas, no doubt influenced by local attitudes. Despite this we did kiss and cuddle, but I felt very guilty about it. I decided that should we kiss again, then I would have to ask her to marry me. She, of course, knew nothing about any of this as it was all in my head. We did kiss again and I did not ask her to marry me, but this was going to have consequences later on in my life. Shortly after this we stopped going out as a couple, but remained friends throughout her stay in Cyprus and beyond.

I am still in touch with one of the airmen, Philip Wade Smith, who arrived on the island in November 1954. He has reminded me that he met up with us at one of our open-air meetings, and he remembers that I taught him to drive. He also says that he once organised a football match and I insisted on driving around the field, to his annoyance, but I have to confess that I have no recollection of such untoward behaviour!

When I settled in England I was invited to his home, but then completely lost touch with him until one day by an extraordinary coincidence we met again. He was working for the Department of Social Security in Colchester, but was seconded to Nottingham and deputed to visit Mutti on behalf of the department. He had not realised whom he was going to see, so was as surprised as we were when we answered the door.

Another interesting man who started coming to the Bible studies was George Burton. I met him at a musical evening at the Anglican archdeacon's house, so my rigid exclusivity may have slipped a bit by then. I never found out what his job was as he never spoke about it, but I think he might have worked in a detention centre. He regularly attended the Bible studies and I spent quite a lot of time with him as he was trying to do an Emmaus Bible study course. He was keen on working with Rev. David Sheppard at the Mayflower Family Centre in Canning Town, London on his return to England.

I think I was introduced to the musical evenings by Peter Sherman, a young man who had a very serious heart defect. It did not stop him cycling and living life to the full. He married after I had left the island, but sadly died young.

I had felt at one point that to be civilised and educated one had to like classical music. My first classical record was Beethoven's *Violin Concerto* (which I still think is wonderful). I added a few more over time, and they proved useful at the archdeacon's musical evenings.

19

The Coming of Change

The Brethren in Nicosia were on the strict side, but there was also warmth and a family atmosphere. In retrospect I did not have a bad life in Cyprus, but I started to feel trapped and wanted out, though the way forward was not immediately clear.

However, having supplied the NAAFI for a few months, by the spring and summer of 1956 we had enough money to be able to consider going to Vienna. Business was slacker in the hot season, so it was the right time to choose. My dad was very ill by this time and desperate to see Vienna again. He also had a lot of faith in Viennese doctors and hoped that they might be able to help him. He had said to me that it was only a matter of time before they devised an operation to deal with angina and he was right, for stents and bypass surgery are now common. Sadly he did not live to see the day.

Flying in those days was still prohibitively expensive and so the three of us travelled by boat and train to Vienna. We sailed from Cyprus on the *Achilleus* on 14th July 1956. Tilda and the others continued to use our house for the meetings and we also left the car so that someone could use it.

We first docked at Piraeus and managed to get to Athens by public transport. We then sailed via Brindisi to Venice and there entrained for Vienna, arriving on 20th July. My father rented reasonably priced accommodation in the Unterer Viaduct Strasse. He was so pleased to be back. I can remember walking (or perhaps more likely crawling) home with him. He did not like people knowing that he had angina pain, so he tried to stop at shop windows or otherwise appear to be doing something until the pain abated. I wish we had taken a taxi. No doubt we thought it too much of a luxury or too expensive.

The Café Herrenhof was still open then, but although I was able to see its size, sadly the large rooms were not filled with guests. Naturally we went and had our meals there and I can remember they made a delicious rice pudding drenched in raspberry juice.

This was my first visit to Vienna since 1938 and I was very impressed, particularly with the wonderful sculptures based on the labours of Hercules at the Michaelerplatz. I am sure my dad would have shown these to me with pride. One evening we were walking along the Ringstrasse near the Municipality or Rathaus, a magnificent building in Gothic style. There were celebrations with music and people dancing in the street and square. My dad was so thrilled to be able to show this to me as it no doubt reminded him of how things used to be.

Nevertheless, what I really wanted was to go to England and it was agreed that I should go for a short visit and leave my parents in Vienna. Except when I had been with my parents, I had never seen big stations with multiple platforms. At one interchange I left my suitcase on the platform and wandered off, perhaps to the toilet. When I returned I could not remember which platform I was on and panicked a bit. To my relief I finally found the right place and my luggage in time to catch the train!

At Victoria Station in London I had a very pleasant experience. I was struggling across the concourse with my belongings when a lady came over and helped me carry them. It was a good introduction to England.

I wrote at least two letters to Mutti, and from these it seems that I spent the first few days at my nurse friend's home in Putney. I also travelled to south Wales to meet Lisa, only to discover that she had left. I did meet up with her somewhere and was also able to see Peter Grosvenor, as well as the Kasparians, who at that time were living in Exeter. I finally ended up with the Kendals, the army doctor and his family who I knew from Limassol, in London.

I knew that my dad had been admitted to hospital but I thought this was for investigations, so it was a shock to be told by the Kendals that he had died of a heart attack on 23rd August. The only blessing was that Lisa and her son Frank had got to Vienna before his death, so they were able to see each other. I was, of course, upset and made arrangements to return to Vienna, crossing to Holland to catch a night train.

I remember nothing of my arrival in Vienna or the funeral. Dad was buried with his sister Martha, whose married name was Rehm. The grave is situated against the rear wall of the huge cemetery and its location is *Group* 107, *Row* 12, *Number* 26.[56] The cemetery now has an internal bus service and there is a stop not too far from the grave.

After Daddy's death we all stayed in Vienna until, I think, the end of September. I cannot recall any particular feelings from that time. In fact the whole period between then and finally coming to England at the end of 1957 is strangely vague and mixed up in my mind.

It is sad that our first post-war visit to Vienna – and indeed the only one for my dad – ended in his death. I am nevertheless glad that he was able to return and to see the place which for him, despite everything that had happened, was home and must have held happy memories pre 1938. I am also glad that it was possible for him to be buried in the same grave as his only sister in the Christian part of the cemetery. I hope and pray that my dad is now in Heaven and that I will be with him there.

We returned to Cyprus early in October 1956, having spent around £253 on our trip to Europe, a significant sum in those days. Lisa and Shane returned to live in Cyprus in the same month, renting a house near us which had a lovely large veranda where one could sit in the cool of the evening. Lisa was a proficient secretary and soon got a job with the government. Their five-year-old son Frank went to a local school. When he came home he was hungry and enjoyed the chocolate wafers. He was a very sweet child.

Lisa enjoyed her social life and tried to get me to go to parties with her as I think she felt I was missing out. I was usually reluctant, but I did go to one where they seemed to spend the whole of the evening playing Bill Haley and His Comets' *Rock Around the Clock*. After a few hours of hearing this song I got used to it and learned at least the first few words.

Nineteen fifty-seven was a critical year. I had lost my dad, but had a law degree and wanted to complete my legal education. However, whichever branch of the profession I chose to aim for, it meant being in or at least visiting England.

---

56 The right to the grave has to be renewed every ten years.

One thing that worried me about settling in England was conscription. I was of the opinion that one might be called up until the age of twenty-six years. In fact I was only twenty-five when I settled in London but was never called up.

Becoming a solicitor seemed out of the question financially. I knew I would have to do articles which meant being in England full-time, and I thought I might have to pay a premium or not get any salary at all. The Bar seemed to present fewer problems as, once enrolled by an Inn of Court, one merely had to keep ten to twelve terms by eating three dinners in hall each term and pass the examinations. It was theoretically possible, therefore, to only be in England four times a year for a few days at a time. We felt that this might be a way forward because we hoped that by me getting a job or continuing to help run the business, we would earn enough to pay the fares.

It was a very confusing period. On 1st December 1956 I entered into a partnership with Mutti, hoping no doubt that business would continue at the same level. Despite this, by about the middle of that month I applied for a job with the Cyprus Civil Service, but was unsuccessful.

In March 1957 I applied to be admitted to the Middle Temple, describing myself as a managing partner. However, even though we were such a tiny business the Inn objected because they thought my position might give me an unfair advantage if I went into legal practice. It was actually a laughable objection as we had no clout and it would have been unlikely that I would have practised in Cyprus anyway. I cannot remember exactly what we decided but I think the upshot was that Mutti would run the business and I would go to England, eat my dinners and return to help her. We did not dissolve the partnership, but whether this was deliberate or an oversight I cannot now say.

I left for England on 4th May. Ten days later I wrote a letter to the Middle Temple saying that from 4th May 1957 I had ceased to be a managing partner and had no gainful occupation whatsoever. I was admitted to the Middle Temple on 20th May. When, about forty-eight years later, I reviewed my 1957 letter I was not entirely happy with what I had said. However, when I wrote to the Middle Temple they in effect told me not to worry about it.

Despite the registered partnership, I tried to get a job in England. Presumably had I been successful I would not have returned to Cyprus, except perhaps to wind things up. I applied to the Overseas Civil Service, but after making a terrible mess of my final interview, was decisively turned down in July 1957. I was terribly upset and it took quite a long time to get over it. I had no option but to return to Cyprus.

On 17th October of that year I again applied for a job with the Cyprus Civil Service. In this application I said that I was self-employed until April 1957 and then studying at the Bar from May, which ties in with what I said to the Middle Temple.

Nothing is as one expects. Mutti decided that she needed to go back to Vienna to sort out the affairs at the Café Herrenhof, and around September she left for Vienna which meant I was on my own with the business. My heart was no longer in it, for all I wanted was to get away from the island and settle in England. In late autumn I wrote to Mutti, telling her that I was going to sell the machinery as best as I could. Mutti was not enraptured with the idea as she thought we had a thriving business – a view apparently reinforced by Mrs Tauber, who by now had settled back in Vienna. I, however, felt that I had a better future in England and I also thought that flying back and forth was just going to be too expensive.

In one of the letters which passed between us there is an interesting snippet as I told Mutti that I had started a Sunday school at home and that about ten children were coming. I can remember how difficult I found it to try to teach them to sing choruses as I had such a bad singing voice!

Anyway, I sold what I could, prepared a final account as of 18th November 1957 and the partnership was dissolved with effect from that date. Maria, who had helped Colin and me when we were making sugar whistles, was still working for us and continued to work for Lisa until she too finally left Cyprus to return to England.

I had written to Mutti to say that I thought I would have our two cats put down, though it made me unhappy. The cats, however, were cleverer than me, for both disappeared the day I was leaving. Although Lisa tried to find them, she never saw them again. Hopefully they had gone into the prison which was located opposite our house and made friends with the prisoners or wardens.

I left it till the last minute to let the landlord know I was leaving. Over the years I have felt guilty about this as I left the property in a poor state, particularly in areas where we had been manufacturing. In 1971 when I was on holiday in Cyprus with Wendy and Mutti I went to meet him in Limassol to give him an opportunity to raise the matter, and actually mentioned it to him myself. He was very friendly and there was no suggestion that he wanted anything from me, which relieved me.

Shortly before leaving Cyprus I bought myself quite a good camera. I had a suspicion that this might be liable to customs duty and decided I would wear it prominently but not actually declare it. I suppose I must have looked very suspicious because a customs officer questioned me about it and then made me pay an import duty of some £30. I am still not sure whether I was liable, but I paid up like a lamb.

My airline ticket to London with KLM was booked via Athens and Vienna. In Athens there was a strike and KLM put me up in a very good hotel for a night. This gave me the opportunity to visit the Acropolis and also see the Olympic Stadium and the palace, which had a ceremonial guard of traditionally dressed Greek soldiers. I would have liked the strike to last a bit longer so that I could continue to enjoy my paid-for holiday!

I have often wondered what Mutti did for money while she lived in Vienna during this period. I cannot remember whether I left some of the sales proceeds with her, but common sense suggests that I would have done. Even so, would it have been enough?

I was very relieved to leave Cyprus at last. Besides having felt stifled there and seeing no future for myself, the hand-to-mouth existence which we had experienced for so many years made me feel that I never wanted to run my own business again.

It was good to settle in England.

Additional Stories

20

The Story of Tante Cilka and the Nuns

Over the years I came across several relatives, or in one case someone connected to a relative who had survived the war in Austria or countries occupied by the Nazis. I thought their stories were interesting and want to share them with you.

Tante Cilka 1955

Tante Cilka,[57] as she was always known to me, was a younger sister of my maternal grandmother. She was born into a large family on 9th July 1884 in Sered, Hungary. At some point she moved and settled in Vienna.

Little is now known of her early life. She married an engineer called Rudolf Koeppel[58] and had one son, Georg,[59] who became an electrical engineer. She apparently owned a pyjama shop in Vienna,[60] but whether this was before or after her husband's death is not known. Georg had emigrated to France, and after the Nazi annexation of Austria in 1938 she followed him there.

Prior to this in 1933 an event occurred in France which was to have momentous implications for Tante Cilka. Mother Benoit Leroy, Mother Superior of a Benedictine nunnery at Jouarre, authorised the founding of a new Benedictine community at Oulchy, which is located north of Paris near Soissons. In 1938 Mother Cecile Nicolle became prioress.

Prioress Cecile Nicholle

---

57 Cecilie or Cecile Koeppel, née Klug.
58 Believed to have been born 10th August 1883. Married 18th April 1909; died in Vienna in 1930.
59 Born 24th November 1912.
60 It is thought at Lenaugasse or Laudongasse.

On 3rd September 1939 Germany declared war on France and invaded on 10th May 1940. On 22nd June Marshal Pétain (the victor at Verdun in the First World War) signed the surrender. The Germans controlled about three fifths of the country and the rest was unoccupied. It was administered by Pétain from Vichy, but was what I would call a vassal state and collaborated with the Germans.

It did not take long for the French authorities in Vichy to enact anti-Jewish legislation. Non-French Jews were to be handed over to the Germans and I understand that some French Jews suffered the same fate. There was a holding camp at Drancy near Paris where Jews were held prior to deportation.

I have ascertained through a BBC programme[61] that the initial deportations from France had not permitted the inclusion of children and so a large number, about four thousand I think, were separated from their parents when their parents were deported. During the programme Odette Baltroff Baticle, who had also been interned at Drancy, spoke about these children. Within a few months the children themselves were also sent to Auschwitz.

Tante Cilka was not, it seems, detained at Drancy. Somehow, she managed to escape, possibly by not reporting[62] for collection, and going into hiding.

However, Tante Cilka and her son Georg were separated. It is known that Georg was detained in Drancy. I had understood that he chose not to escape the Nazis with his mother because, he was working with children and did not want to leave them. On the other hand it may be that, being in custody, he could not escape.[63]

Georg lost his life, for he was deported to Auschwitz from Drancy on 17th August 1942. He was located in Wagon 6 of the train. I wonder whether some of the children sent to Drancy were on the same train?[64]

Things were not good for the Benedictine nuns either. The Germans requisitioned their abbey at Oulchy and in 1940 they fled to the south of France, settling at Touscayrats in Vichy France. This was hundreds

---

61   BBC 2, 19th November 2005; *Auschwitz:The Nazis and the Final Solution*.
62   Email from Annie Parolini, a niece of Tante Cilka's, 21st May 2006.
63   The latter view being that of Annie Parolini.
64   Information from Diane Afoumado, then of Memorial de la Shoah.

of kilometres away from Oulchy, but had the advantage that it was near another monastery which was quite large and situated at Dourgne. The nearest bigger town was Albi.

In the meanwhile, Tante Cilka remained in hiding. Somehow she made her way to the south of France and family lore had it that she hid in the vineyards for some of the time at least. Despite all her efforts it could only have been a matter of time before the Vichy French or the Germans would have found her. I suppose that the risk would have increased following 11th November 1942 when the Germans invaded Vichy France.[65]

Around the time of the invasion, the Bishop of Albi, Monsignor Moussaron, asked the nuns at Touscayrats to take Tante Cilka and another lady known as Madame Rose into safekeeping. I think it must be a reasonable assumption that if the bishop knew about them then so must other ordinary French people in and around Albi, but it would seem that no one gave them away to the authorities.

Quite how long Tante Cilka was on the run is not clear, but it is likely to have been several weeks. I was told that according to the records, she and Madame Rose were received into the community on 6th October 1942. The records speak of one of the refugees having spent several weeks on the run, taking refuge in an attic, whilst the other was more recently pursued. The one on the run I think was Tante Cilka, for even if we date her escape into hiding from as late as the date of Georg's deportation in August 1942, several weeks elapsed before she was received by the abbey.

I have been told that the bishop asked the nuns[66] to take the two refugees at the time when the invasion occurred. From the dates it is clear that the ladies were received before the actual invasion, but it may well be that there were warning signs that something was about to happen. Touscayrats was chosen because the bishop must have thought that it offered the maximum degree of security for the women. They would

---

65   www.historylearningsite.co.uk/french_resistance.htm

66   The French term is *moniales*, which implies a contemplative or enclosed community, but I will use the word 'nun' as it is more readily understood in English. There seem to be three kinds of Roman Catholic nuns: apostolic (working in the professions, e.g. hospitals or schools), missionary (spreading the gospel) and enclosed or contemplative (who pray for the world).

have disappeared from sight altogether once in the community, and I suppose people who had known of them might well have assumed that they had either been caught, or moved on to another area.

It must be stressed that the nuns took a considerable personal risk in accepting these two refugees, for if they had been discovered, there can be little doubt that they too would have suffered severely for sheltering them. It says much for them that they did so and that no one broke ranks for all the war years. It has been pointed out to me that the reason why they were prepared to take the risk was because of the words of Jesus such as *That you love one another as I have loved you*[67] and *in as much as you have done it to the least of these my brethren ye have done it unto me.*[68]

Mother Cecile arranged for the two ladies to have a large room. They were certainly not prisoners but, initially at least, they were told not to come out of their room for reasons of safety.

Meeting medical needs was a problem. While it would have been possible to get a doctor to call within the abbey confines, dentistry would have presented greater problems because of the need for instruments and would usually have meant a visit in town or to Dourgne.

I was told by my Aunt Edith that seeing a dentist was a most welcome experience after the war for Tante Cilka, so presumably there were needs which could not have been met at the time.

No doubt the life of Benedictine nuns went on as normally as possible with the observations of the offices. I imagine that attendance of these was voluntary for Tante Cilka, but it may well be that she did go at least sometimes.

There do not seem to be any records that searches took place, but on one occasion, a German soldier did come to the abbey. It is not clear what the purpose of his visit was, but the nun who received him played dumb and in the end showed him into the chapel. He presumably left with no harm done.

It is very difficult to imagine what it must have been like for Tante Cilka, her fellow refugee and the nuns to be living in a situation where they knew that if they were discovered, all would be over. That the risk of betrayal was well known will become evident in a moment. In addition,

67 Authorised version, John 13.34.
68 Authorised version, Matthew 25.35.

Tante Cilka probably would not have known what had happened to her only son, and the pain and anguish of this must have been considerable.

On 2nd March (this was before D-Day) the property at Touscayrats was to be requisitioned and the nuns would have to leave in three days, moving to the monastery or abbey at Dourgne. This monastery, which had been a help and support to the nuns, now became a refuge for them and for others too, which meant that it was overcrowded. Because of the presence of so many people and the consequent risk of betrayal, Mother Cecile Nicolle felt that it was not safe to take the two refugee ladies with them. She therefore decided that the safest course was to leave them behind in the care of Sister Aguilberte.

The archives record that the parting on this day was not easy for either the refugees or the nuns, with *heartbreaking goodbyes from these poor ladies, whose affection and gratitude burst out, and who have moving words and gestures.*[69]

Tante Cilka's address to Mother Cecile Nicolle is also recorded:

"My heart is very happy for you because at Dourgne at least you have times of rest and less worry, more than of my suffering I think of your welfare"

To prove this she offered Mother Cecile Nicolle a valuable ring which she still had, to help the nuns, forgetting her own needs and distressing situation. Mother Cecile Nicolle was very touched but refused to accept it.

It may be that the Germans were not moving in just yet and that is why it was possible to leave the refugees with a nun at Touscayrats. In any event on 7th March 1944 Mother Cecile Nicolle returned to Touscayrats to try to sort things out because of the urgency and the distressing situation which everyone was in, particularly the precarious position of Tante Cilka and Madame Rose.

Because of the risk of betrayal at Dourgne, arrangements were made for the temporary reception of the refugees into an order of Apostolic nuns located in Albi, named Les Soeurs du Bon Sauveur (Sisters of our Good Saviour). The Mother Superior of this community was Madame Batut.

It is not entirely clear whether the refugees were living within the community house or in separate dwellings in the town under the care and

---

69   This and other quotations are translations of what is in the records.

protection of this order. It was felt that a bigger town like Albi gave a degree of protection in itself, but even so these nuns were taking the same risk as the Benedictine nuns had done.

On 7th July the Benedictine community again moved, this time to Neuvic where Tante Cilka and her companion rejoined them. This suggests that they were hidden in Albi for at least three months.

I imagine if the farewells in March were painful, the reunion must have been great. Also by this time the Allies had landed in Normandy and I expect that people knew that the end of the war was approaching.

The situation at Neuvic was grim. It was cold, wet because the roof leaked, and there was very little food. They had to try to gather wood for fire as best as they could. On top of this, they no longer had the support of the Dourgne community and were cast entirely upon themselves because of the considerable distance between Dourgne and Neuvic. Furthermore, there was no work and they had no money.

The war finally ended on 8th May 1945. France had been liberated prior to that, so the danger from the Germans had passed and Tante Cilka had survived thanks to the nuns who had risked so much for her.

Having spent just over a year at Neuvic, on 25th July the community moved back to their original home at Oulchy. Conditions here were not much better than at Neuvic because the monastery had been devastated by the war.

Tante Cilka was of course now free to go, but it is not clear when she actually left the community. Madame Rose disappears from the records and the community do not know what became of her.

On 30th August 1947 Tante Cilka is recorded as being with the nuns at Oulchy. She may well have just returned for a visit as there is a reference to lady guests including her.

This was an important time for the nuns for they were on retreat, which was being led by Father Thomas d'Aquin of the Pierre qui Vire. The subject was *The Fatherhood of God*, and the preaching was much appreciated. It is described as clear, strong and unforgettable, and Tante Cilka is said to have *found there light, love and happiness*. It would seem that during this time Tante Cilka expressed a wish to be baptised. That is not surprising as she had seen the nuns in action and it may be that the preaching at the retreat had also stirred her heart.

However, apparently Father Thomas advised her against baptism as he felt that she would reintegrate better with the Jewish community if she did not take this step. I am amazed at this advice, for as I understand Roman Catholic doctrine, baptism is considered a very important and possibly vital step, and so for a priest to advise against it at that time must have been very unusual. However, I remember Mutti telling me that Tante Cilka was a Roman Catholic, which did not surprise me in view of her good experiences within the community of nuns during and after the war.

On 14th September 1947 there is a reference to Tante Cilka thinking of emigrating to America. She is recorded as saying goodbye with regrets on all sides, and is described as a Christian in heart and spirit but without being baptised. However, it took several years before she was actually able to leave.

In 1948 the community again moved to La Loyère, near Chalon-sur-Saône. This move does not seem to have improved the lot of the sisters as the property was surrounded by a water-filled moat where midges bred and are said to have tormented the nuns. In addition the hygiene conditions were bad and cooking facilities were underground and poor. They stuck it out there until 1963 when they found a permanent home at Venière.

On 1st August 1948 Tante Cilka visited La Loyère, and again on 6th November. The nuns obviously thought that she was on her way to America for they wondered if they would ever see her again.

This too, however, proved a false departure because on 13th February 1949 there is another entry saying Tante Cilka departs for America, but on 30th October 1949 poor Tante Cilka is still waiting for her passport.

The last time she is recorded as visiting La Loyère is on 4th July 1950. On this occasion a sister with artistic abilities named Sister Marie-Madeleine Augé made two drawings of her, copies of which have been given to us. We met this sister in June 2005. She has written a eulogy which reads as follows:

She was a very refined person of deep spirituality, she showed immense gratitude to those who had saved her by welcoming her like a sister and by concealing her at their own risk and perils from searches by the Gestapo. I was able to do this sketch during her stay at La Loyère around 1949–50.

Sketches of Tante Cilka by Sister Marie-Madeleine Augé

Tante Cilka was much loved and respected by the community, for they describe her as a friend of the monastery and of every one of the nuns.

By 1951 at last Tante Cilka was settled in New York in the Jewish community. I understand that this was organised by her step-nephew Lipod who was living in the States already.

The Jewish National Fund has a tree-planting programme near Jerusalem and Tante Cilka planted a tree there in honour of Mother Cecile Nicolle, a little plaque commemorating the fact.[70] She kept up a correspondence with Cecile Nicolle for as long as possible.

She also wrote to Sister Aguilberte, with whom she had become friends. This was the sister who had been left behind to look after the ladies at Touscayrats.

On 12th October 1991 the sisters at Venière received a letter or card from Tante Cilka which had been found among the possessions of Sister Aguilberte. The missive was almost certainly sent from the USA. It included a comment: *everything is very bad for me here.* It is sad that that should be the last entry in the community records.

In this communication Tante Cilka apparently also mentions that out of the fourteen families of her brothers and sisters she only had one sister-in-law and three nephews surviving. It would seem that Tante Cilka had forgotten some other relatives such as Annie Parolini and Mutti, who

---

70   Could be at Yad Vashem.

were still alive at that time. However, there can be little doubt that a large number of family members were lost in the Holocaust. Tante Edith said she (and I suspect also Uncle Hans) had worked out that sixty-six members of the family perished.

In 1969 Wendy, the children (three at that time) and I went to Canada and stayed with Wendy's sister Shirley. While we were there I said that as New York seemed only a hop away on the map, could we go to visit my great-aunt? We went on the train and it proved a very long hop!

Tante Cilka was living in an apartment in a rather run-down area of Harlem. She must have been around eighty-five years old. Sadly I can remember next to nothing about seeing her. Wendy remembers her better and recalls a sprightly old lady.

It would seem that she spent her last years in a rest home called Home and Hospital in the Bronx. Tante Edith remembers that she must have died in her sleep for she did not come down to breakfast and was found dead in bed.

I was able to ascertain from Annie Parolini that the date of death was 29th June 1975.[71] Annie and her step-nephew Lipod attended the funeral and Annie paid for the perpetual care of her grave and for grass seeds and topsoil.

Tante Cilka was a gifted artist and Annie has some of her drawings. I have been able to obtain a couple, which are reproduced here.

You may well ask how I know all this.

In November 2004 I went to Vienna for a short visit and, among other things, went to the Jewish part of the main cemetery to see my paternal grandparents' grave site, which we had only just recently identified. While there I also saw the grave where Grete Rappaport (née Klug) was buried. The person in the office gave me the telephone number and address of Annie Parolini, Grete's sister in America. On the off chance that she was still alive I phoned, and indeed she was, and gave me her email address. I asked her about Tante Cilka and she told me that she had been in touch with her.

Then out of the blue she sent me an email saying she had found an old address book containing an address for Mother Cecile Nicolle: Abbey St.

---

71   Tante Cilka was buried at Floral Park Cemetery (Washington Cemetery), 104 Deans Rhode Hall Road, Monmouth Junction NJ 08852 (Section 2, Block 2, Lots 11–12, Grave 115, Map 20).

Two drawings by Tante Cilka. Subjects not known

Michael Kergonan, Morbihan, which I misread as Morlilau. I followed this up and eventually found out the present address of the community who had taken Tante Cilka in. It was the Abbey of Notre Dame, Venière 71700, Boyer, France. I wrote to them and received lots of information from the abbess and Sister Marguerite Marie, the archivist.

In June 2005 Wendy, Lisa and I went and stayed in their visitor accommodation. The sisters could not have been kinder or more helpful, and we were lucky in that there was a Swiss-German sister called Michael who spoke very good German (much better than I did) and some English.

We spent several hours with them, spread over several days. They showed us lovely photograph albums from 1933 onward. The pages were decorated with drawings showing some background information. There was also an album which the nuns had presented to their abbess on 8th September 1998, the twenty-seventh anniversary of her becoming abbess. This volume had many quotations taken from Saint-Exupéry, the man who wrote *The Little Prince*.

On the Friday of our visit after vespers, the abbess arranged for us to meet most of the nuns including the sisters who could remember Tante Cilka. There were five of them, four from the war years and another from one of the post-war visits. One was a hundred years old.

It is amazing when one considers the risks of hiding Tante Cilka and Madame Rose that any entries about them were made in the archives at all. It stands to reason that had they had to be produced, they would have been very incriminating documents indeed.

21

Tante Martha

Tante Martha

My father had one sister, Martha, born on 6th April 1900.[72] She was a friend of Mutti's and it was as a result of that friendship that Mutti met Dad and got married.

Sadly after we left Vienna in 1938 I never saw Tante Martha again and have no visual memories of her, but do remember that I was fond of her. I have tried to piece together her story based on family lore and research. It is tantalisingly sketchy, but the best I could do.

I understand that in Vienna it was a legal requirement that people registered their address. Using a reference book and a local authority source[73] in Vienna I have tried to trace my aunt's movements.

By all accounts Tante Martha was glamorous, a gifted pianist, and a good enough dancer to have her own dance school. She moved several times but by 1938 was located at Oppolzergasse 4, which was an upmarket address near the opera. Maybe because of her connection with Mutti, she also had the use of the dance hall at the Café Herrenhof.

As a result of her dance activities, Tante Martha met Edgar Rehm,[74] a young student lawyer from a Roman Catholic family. His father had been a marine officer and he was registered as living with his widowed mother, Emma.

On 5th June 1930 Martha and Edgar married in a civil ceremony, which was only possible because both declared themselves as being without religious belief. It is difficult to work out whether they lived together and if so where. For five years after the marriage Tante Martha remained registered at her parents' address[75] whilst Edgar continued to live at his mother's address, although his registration certificate was amended to refer to Tante Martha. Whether that meant that she actually lived with him there, I do not know.

For some years Edgar worked in Baden, a small town near Vienna, and I suspect that Tante Martha also spent time there for on 15th March 1934 the district court in Baden granted a judicial separation, or as it was known, a 'divorce from table and bed'. It might therefore appear that this was just another short-lived unhappy marriage with the parties

---

72 2 Westbahnhofstrasse 23, but the family moved to 2 Taborstrasse 66 Vienna at some point.
73 Lehman and local authority Mag 8.
74 Date of birth: 30th October 1896.
75 Taborstrasse 66.

going their separate ways, but as will be seen, the evidence is against that.

Tante Martha was baptised into the Roman Catholic faith on 28th April 1934 at a rather beautiful church called Pfarrkirche St. Leopold.[76] Her added baptismal name was her mother's name, Anna. It is strange that this ceremony took place just a few days after the judicial separation. Why on earth would Tante Martha have done that? It is of course possible that she took this step because of conviction, and I would like to think that this is so. Or was it that she was trying to save the marriage, make things easier for Edgar job-wise, or perhaps make herself more acceptable to her husband's family? Again it may be that, having seen what was happening next door in Germany, she thought it was a sensible thing to do, particularly as she had already renounced her Jewish faith.

On 12th March 1938 the Nazis annexed Austria. Tante Martha had already lost her dad to heart disease in 1936, but her mother Anna had continued to live in the family home at 66 Taborstrasse. Sadly, six days after the annexation Anna took her own life while staying at her daughter's flat. I had always understood that she had jumped from a window, but the records indicate an overdose of the barbiturate Veronal, which I believe in those days was sometimes used as a sleeping drug.

It was a drastic step to take! Perhaps Anna was one of the Jewish people who were forced to clean up the streets, or had seen it happen. Coincidentally, Edgar, though never a member of the Nazi Party, had made a commitment of allegiance to Hitler on that very day and that might have been the last straw. We will never know for sure the reason for Anna's action, but given the timing we have been told that she is classed as a victim of the Holocaust.

She was buried with her husband in the Jewish part of the Central Cemetery in Vienna.[77] When I was in Austria in 2004 I found their grave, which was in a terrible state of devastation with no memorial stone. I got a local stonemason to tidy up the site, and then in 2008 my wife Wendy and I had a small memorial erected for them.

After the Nazi annexation it was not uncommon for divorces to take place when the spouses were Jewish. I suspect non-Jewish partners may

---

76   Alexander-Poch-Platz 6, 1020 Vienna 2.
77   The grave reference is Group 22, Row 18, Number 25. Entrance to this
       part of the cemetery is gained via Gate 4.

have been pressurised into taking this step for the sake of their careers. There were in fact major advantages to Jewish partners if the marriage persisted because it seems that the Nazis did not deport them as long as the non-Jewish partners were alive. Maybe this was not fully understood in 1938.

As Martha and Edgar were already judicially separated it is not surprising that they went ahead with the divorce.[78] Although couples divorced it did not always follow that they actually broke up, and this may have applied in this case too.

If one pauses for a moment to review Tante Martha's situation in 1938, things must have been awful. In her own home, she lost her mother through suicide. She and her husband divorced. Her only brother and his immediate family left Austria in August of that year, so as far as family was concerned she was left destitute. On top of that, she probably would not have been able to use the Café Herrenhof after about the 15th March 1938 as the owners were barred from it, so her livelihood might also have been affected.

In the light of all this, one would have imagined that she would want to leave Vienna if she had the opportunity. I have no documentary evidence for this, but Tante Edith has told me that my dad managed to get Martha an entry permit to Cyprus. However, she refused to go, the reason apparently being that she was married to a magistrate who she got to know at the dance school. This surely cannot be anyone else other than Edgar. I find it very difficult to understand Tante Martha's reluctance to leave unless the judicial separation and divorce were just a charade so as not to hinder Edgar's good career prospects.

Another odd fact which may be a pointer that there was still a relationship is that the dance school was registered in the names of Rehm and Popper between 1936 and 1940 before reverting to the sole name of Popper for the period 1940–1942.

From registration records it seems Tante Martha moved out of Oppolzergasse on 17th October 1938. From that date till 28th May 1942 she lived at seven named addresses. Not all would have been with Jewish householders as only two of the landlords refer to the people who use the name Israel or Sara, a compulsory addition to your name if you were

---

78 In Vienna on 19th October 1938 and effective from 5th December.

Jewish. Some of the stays were of short duration, probably wisely as the vast majority of the people who lived in the same blocks as Tante Martha were deported and most of those are recorded as having died.

On 28th May 1942 she moved from an address where the landlady was Jewish and disappeared. She reappeared on 6th June 1945 and the records shows her at an address at 9 Porzellangasse 43/3/23, where she only stayed for one day. She then moved again, and finally on 6th July 1945 moved to 3 Reisnerstrasse 15/3, which was Edgar's address. I feel sure that she remained there until her death.

What had happened to her, then, during the three years from 1942 to 1945?

After the war someone called Hugo Glaser formed a 'U-boot association'. 'U-boot' – or its English equivalent, 'U-boat' – is the term coined to describe people who went underground and vanished from the public gaze.

I have located a registration card relating to Tante Martha which states specifically that she was a 'U-boat' from 1942–1945. This document describes her occupation as *knitter*. I have not been able to find out anything else, either about the organisation or Tante Martha's involvement with it.

We will never know for sure and there are other possibilities, but I think it is a reasonable assumption that she was hidden, for all or part of this time, at Edgar's home.

Edgar's mother was buried on 10th September 1942. Tante Martha's disappearance started about three months prior to her death. In view of Emma's age, necessity may have made it expedient for Tante Martha to move in with her and look after her. Whatever the situation prior to Emma's death, the flat was likely to have been empty thereafter as Edgar was in France with the German Air Force. It would therefore have been available for Martha to continue to live there, and given their subsequent history this makes sense to me. This also seems to be the opinion of someone at the Document Archive of the Austrian Resistance (DOEW)[79].

There are, however, several obvious puzzles. Why did she not reappear immediately after the war ended? Why is it that on her reappearance she is registered at two other addresses before ending up at Edgar's? Both of these suggest that she was hidden elsewhere, unless perhaps this was a

---

79 Now also known as the DOW – Dokumentationsarchiv des österreichischen Wilderstandes

177

device to hide what had actually happened. On the other hand the U-boat registration card shows her at Edgar's home, and the date against that entry is 6th June 1945, the date of reappearance.

If I am right about where she was hidden, there would have been a risk to Edgar during the Nazi era if it were to become known that he had given shelter to his former wife. What name she used and what other steps Edgar may have taken to protect her or himself are now impossible to say. It is intriguing to speculate, but I fear it will not provide answers.

Now for a little bit more about Edgar, who was the son of Otto Rehm,[80] a captain of a frigate in the Austrian-Hungarian Navy, and Emma Maria Hilda, née von Wolf.[81] Edgar fought in the First World War and was decorated. He studied law and passed his judge's exams in 1924 with an award of 'very good'.

In post-Nazi annexation documentation he confirms that he had been married, but says he was divorced from March 1934, which in fact was only the date of the judicial separation.

In August 1939 he applied for a promotion in the judicial hierarchy. There were no adverse comments about his political position, which was a necessary prerequisite if he was to get advancement. The appointment was granted in the name of Hitler in March 1940. Almost immediately afterwards Edgar was called up to serve as a lieutenant in the German Air Force with effect from 30th April 1940, first in Germany and then in France. He did quite well and was twice promoted and also decorated. It therefore seems unlikely to me that Edgar was present in the flat for most of the war years.

Edgar had never joined the Nazi Party. This meant that after the war he was eligible for judicial appointment and rose to the position of Advocate General in Vienna (*Generalstadtsanwalt*).

Soon after the war ended Martha and Edgar re-established contact with my parents. Unfortunately not many letters were kept, but I have found one written in November 1946 from Tabora by my father, addressed in affectionate terms to both his sister and Edgar. He says that three weeks have passed without a letter from them, so the contact must have been in place for some time. The letter is far-ranging, speaking about food parcels which my father is sending and enquiring after his sister's health.

---

80   Born on 19th September 1856 and died 2nd March 1908.
81   Born on 8th May 1875 (?) in Romania.

He also addresses Edgar directly and asks him questions about issues of restitution.

In the late 1940s after protracted negotiations my grandparents again had an interest in the Café Herrenhof. A person of trust and responsibility was sought to look after their interests, and Tante Martha was proposed for this job. She started working at the café and initially at least was rewarded simply with meals for herself and for Edgar, but by 1949 was in receipt of a small salary. It is worth recording that Lisa has seen a letter from Opapa in which he says that the only person who has behaved decently was Tante Martha.

Although I have not been able to find any evidence that Martha and Edgar remarried, our family always considered them as a couple.

There is one final interesting coincidence. During the course of my search for information on Tante Martha I was told about a Mrs Edith Krisch at Bund Sozialistischer Freiheitskämpfer,[82] and it was suggested that she might be able to help. In fact we struck lucky because it turned out that after the war she and her parents knew Tante Martha and Edgar well, and Mrs Krisch says that as far as she can remember Tante Martha and Edgar lived together.

Mrs Krisch's father was a police dog handler and trained the Rehms' dog for them. Her grandmother used to look after it from time to time, and Mrs Krisch, who was only four in 1945, can remember the dog better than anything else. She describes him as a cross-breed with long ears, gentle and affectionate. Her grandmother nicknamed him '*Wotrabek auf the Durchreise*' because he was quite comical-looking. *Durchreise* means 'travelling through', but what *Wotrabek* meant I had no idea and nor had Mrs Krisch. However, Chava Livni[83] thinks that this word is a corruption of the Czech phrase *votrava, otrava otravek*, which means 'pain in the neck'. She points out that many Czech words were adopted into German, and I am sure she is right. That makes the dog's name 'a passing pain in the neck'. Grandma must have had quite a sense of humour!

Mrs Krisch's memories of Tante Martha are sketchy, recalling that she was rather soft with the dog, which the latter exploited! She describes Tante Martha as *herzliche*, which I interpret as 'warm-hearted', and says it was her aim to bring pleasure to the Krisch family. At one time Tante

---

82 Association of Socialist Freedom Fighters.
83 Chava Livni's story appears later.

Martha knitted a red pullover with a light blue pattern out of angora wool for Mrs Krisch. Another memory was of going with her father to visit Tante Martha at the Café Herrenhof where she worked as a cashier. Both Mrs Krisch and her brother have happy memories of the Rehm family.

It is so tantalising to have got close to someone who actually knew Tante Martha in the immediate post-war years, and yet was too young to be able to add details of her survival during the war.

Tante Martha's health was not good. I was told that she suffered kidney disease, which was attributed to the privations she suffered. Also, Tante Edith had mentioned that even when she was young there was some problem with her heart which meant that she had to be careful with energetic dances. It was, of course, the time of the Charleston!

In 1951 things took a terminal turn. On 8th June Mutti got a letter from Tante Edith's sister Melanie Girkmann saying that there were doubts as to Tante Martha's prospects of recovery. The note also says that apart from when at the office Edgar was spending all his time at the hospital, and as a consequence had not been able to reply to Mutti's letter.

Although containing bad news, the letter confirms that Edgar and Tante Martha were close. I have seen a page from a letter by Mutti in which she mentions Melanie's correspondence and says how upset Daddy is that he cannot go to see his sister, owing to lack of finances.

At 18.45 on 12th June 1951 Tante Martha died at the Rudolfstiftung (Rudolf Hospital).[84] Her home address was 3 Reisnerstrasse 15/3, Edgar's address. The primary cause of death seems to have been heart disease, but the presence of kidney disease is also recorded. She was buried at ten o'clock on 19th June in the Christian section of the Central Cemetery in Vienna in a grave purchased by Edgar.[85]

In 1956 when we at last managed to return to Vienna, Daddy died. Mutti got permission from Edgar for him to be buried in the same grave as Tante Martha, and thus brother and sister were reunited in death.

For my seventieth birthday my daughter Sue took me to Vienna. We walked past the memorials of important people like Beethoven and eventually got to my dad's and Tante Martha's grave. I do not recommend the walk as the cemetery is huge, but it is possible to drive into it in a taxi

---

84   Boerhaavegasse 8, 1030 Wien
85   The grave reference is Group 107, Row 12, Number 26.

or catch an internal bus, which in 2008 ran on a free-of-charge basis. There is a stop not far from the grave.

After Tante Martha died we lost regular contact with Edgar. However, whilst researching what had happened to Tante Martha I did learn a little more about him. I came across Mrs Celia Male, and she located Edgar's grave from the cemetery records for me and noted that it was cared for. I wrote to the cemetery authorities and in due course I had a reply from Dr Eva Wagner, who turned out to be the sister of Edgar's second wife Klementine.[86] In 2004 Dr Wagner kindly travelled to meet me at the Hotel Stephanie in Vienna where I was staying. Unfortunately she did not know much about Tante Martha, but told me that Klementine was much younger than Edgar. He had known her pre-war but lost touch. After the war they met again and married. Edgar died on 7th April 1965. His home address was still 3 Reisnerstrasse 15/3. Klementine died some twenty-five years later and was buried with Edgar on 15th November 1990.

---

86 Née Schnitzer.

22

Erich H. Waldmann

Erich playing the piano in flat

Some years ago I renewed contact with Erich Waldmann and met his family. Erich's father Robert, the eldest of eleven children, was my grandfather's brother and so my great-uncle. This large family lived initially in Boesing, now Pezinok in Slovakia, but at that time within the Kingdom of Hungary.

Robert's father Moses, better known as Moritz, had a small all-purpose store in the border town. There was a significant Jewish community with its own synagogue. The Waldmanns had a reputation for longevity and it was rumoured that Erich's great-great-great-grandfather (who had a biblical name; possibly Isaac) is reputed to have died at 120. The family account is that he died in a quasi-biblical setting under a large tree with his family around him. He blessed them, lit his pipe and passed peacefully away. Robert, who was born on 18th July 1869, was aged four at the time.

After attending school, Robert became a trainee in his father's business. However, his dad felt that he belonged in a city and, having given him a leaving certificate, seventeen-year-old Robert moved to Vienna. He loved this city, in particular the culture and the opera. He got a position with textile merchants Reiss and Brett, where he became chief clerk.

His first marriage ended in divorce. There were two children. Paul died in infancy and George moved to London in 1938, but his whereabouts are not known.

Working at Reiss and Brett was a young woman called Anna Antonia Kolitsch.[87] She was Viennese, non-Jewish and a Roman Catholic. She was also joyful and a beautiful blonde, and the couple fell deeply in love. In 1918, despite an age difference of twenty-seven years, they married in the town hall, Anna having converted to Judaism. However, shortly before the birth of their daughter Ilse on 8th August 1920, Anna returned to her Roman Catholic roots so that the child could be christened a Roman Catholic.

In 1924 Anna was pregnant again, this time with Erich. Robert's mother Johanna Waldmann died a month before Erich was born,[88] but she may have made her son promise that if the baby was a boy he would be brought up in the Jewish faith. Whatever the reason, Erich was brought up as a Jew.

And so this family consisted of a full Jewish father, a Gentile mother and two half-Jewish children, one being brought up as a Catholic and the other as a Jew. A real mix. The fact that the two children were brought up in different faiths was to have a profound effect later.

The family was not religious. They observed the principal festivals of

---

87 Born on 6th April 1895, the second of four surviving children.
88 Date of birth: 15th July 1924.

both the Catholic and Jewish faiths and Erich says that he enjoyed being brought up in such a mixed-faith family. The important Jewish festivals including Passover and Yom Kippur (the Day of Atonement) were held at Robert's home as the firstborn sibling living in Vienna.

Erich remembers that they observed various Jewish customs such as having an empty chair at the dinner table at Passover. As the only son of Robert's second marriage, Erich was asked to go to the door to formally check that there was no poor, hungry stranger outside to be invited in to join the Passover meal. Prayers were also said and various other ceremonies observed, such as dipping long white radishes in salt water and eating them with prayers during the meal. But although there was a religious component it was more of a family occasion, with my grandad Bela, my Great-Aunts Sidonie, Eugenie and Bertha, and my Great-Uncles Ernst and Gustav present. It must have been quite a gathering as I assume their children were also there.

The family also observed Christmas and Easter festivities. Friday was a meatless day, which was of course Catholic custom.

Church or synagogue attendance was, for the family sporadic. Erich remembers going to traditional Catholic feast day markets and services, but the thing that sticks in his mind is getting a marzipan sausage known as a *Peregrinkipferl*. However, he was sent for Jewish religious education, had to learn Hebrew and was expected to attend the synagogue.

Because of this mixture of beliefs in the family, Erich remembers a funny episode when he was six. At school, during a religious instruction class for Catholic children, the other children, including Jews and Protestants, were told to leave. Erich presumably had no idea what they were talking about and stayed and listened enthusiastically to the story of a living God and the dear Lord Jesus. When he got home he was all excited and told his mum. She evidently was shocked and told him in future he had to attend the Bible instruction for Jewish children.

After Robert and Anna's wedding in 1918, Robert founded a company dealing in kitchen equipment. Anna did the bookkeeping. They did well initially and even had a car and a chauffeur, which was quite unusual in those days. Unfortunately the recession came, things went from bad to worse and Robert went bankrupt. He tried to continue working from home and was the first person to bring Japanese tea and coffee sets to Vienna. However, despite his best efforts he could not earn enough and Anna had to get a job as a cloakroom attendant at the Café Schottentor, which was owned by other members of the extended Waldmann family.[89]

Things got much worse after 12th March 1938 when Hitler annexed Austria. Jews, who were already discriminated against, in effect now had no rights. Erich recalls that many, including old people, were forced to wash away inscriptions on the streets, though he and his family were spared this. The inscriptions were I think political slogans relating to an election or plebiscite which Schuschnigg, the Chancellor at the time of the annexation, had planned.

The Nazis had a complicated system for determining whether a person was to be classified as a full Jew or as someone of mixed race, and there were two categories for these. Ilse had been baptised as a child and brought up as a Roman Catholic, and because two of her grandparents were non-Jewish she was classed as a Class 1 mixed-race person. I think that the fact that she was baptised a Catholic before the Nuremberg laws in 1935 was significant with regard to her rights. In contrast Erich, with identical blood flowing through his veins but brought up Jewish, was treated as a full Jew. The fact that he was baptised in 1940 made no difference.

The consequences of the distinction were very significant. Ilse was subject to only limited discrimination. For example, she was not allowed to proceed to further education, but she was able to get a job and did not have to wear a Jewish star. She could also go to the cinema or theatre if she wished. Erich, on the other hand, bore the full brunt of Nazi discrimination.

Robert, now sixty-nine, had his small pension further reduced. He was of course the most Jewish of all the family, but he was protected to an extent by the fact that he was married to Anna. As I understand it, Jewish spouses were protected from deportation as long as their non-Jewish partners were alive. Should the partner die, then this protection disappeared and they were liable to be deported forthwith. Of course it is well known that in many cases the parties divorced, which would have robbed the Jewish partner of this protection. My dad's sister Tante Martha Rehm and Aunt Edith's sister Melanie Girkmann were divorced, as will be seen from their stories. It may well have been the case that the Aryan partner was put under pressure, for example with regard to employment

---

89   Eugenie Lichtenstein (née Waldmann) and Ernst and/or Gustav Waldmann.

if they did not dissolve the marriage. In Robert and Anna's case, however, the couple stuck together. The one most at risk was Erich because of his classification as Jewish. I think that the thing that protected him initially at least was his age, as he was only thirteen in 1938 and still at school.

Just a few months after the annexation, Erich became fourteen and withdrew from the Jewish faith. This was the earliest he was allowed to do so. Together with his father he was baptised in the Roman Catholic faith in 1940. Robert and Anna then had to go through another marriage ceremony as Erich says the church would not recognise the validity of the initial Jewish marriage, even though it had been performed in the town hall. Bearing in mind the strict Roman Catholic rules about remarriage following divorce, one must presume that Robert's first wife had by this time passed away. Erich's birth certificate, issued by the Jewish authority,[90] recognised him as the legitimate son of the couple, as does the baptismal certificate, which suggests to me that the 1918 marriage was recognised as valid notwithstanding the requirement to remarry mentioned above.

The family of course tried to rectify the anomalous and ridiculous situation with regard to the two children. Anna had applied to Berlin to have Erich reclassified as mixed-race Class 1 like his sister. The application was not rejected out of hand, but Erich was subjected to various tests including the measurement of physical features such as length of his nose! Finally a reply was received from Goebbels saying the decision would have to wait until 'final victory'. This was tantamount to a refusal and not a good outcome for Erich. He was still considered a Jew, had to wear a Jewish star and was of course always in danger.

I think there can be little doubt that the family would not have survived but for the fact that Anna was non-Jewish. She was able to get a good job as a chief bookkeeper with a Czech purchasing cooperative, and was able to retain this job throughout the war. Her income was more or less sufficient for the family not to have financial worries, but there were of course emotional and spiritual ones.

It would be a mistake to think that there had been no discrimination prior to Hitler's entry into Austria. For example, Jewish children were normally sent to separate schools, though as it happens the Robert Hamerling Gymnasium, the school that Erich attended, was an exception

---

90 Gives his name as Erich Heinz.

until the summer of 1938. However, from 1934 onward the 'A' classes were reserved for Catholic students and the 'B' classes for children who were Jewish, Protestant (called Evangelical in Austria) or who did not have a religious affiliation. Erich, of course, was in the 'B' stream.

Prior to the annexation I believe it was not permitted to be openly a member of the Nazi Party in Austria. Those who had been secret members revealed themselves immediately on Hitler's entry. At Erich's school it turned out that a highly valued English teacher had been one of these. He turned up dressed in SA uniform and gave a fiery speech to the whole school.

Despite this, Erich felt that the teachers behaved properly and remembers in particular the geography and history teacher, Professor Mayer, who said that the only law he adhered to was whether a student was good or bad. Nevertheless, by autumn 1938 the school was closed to Erich and, rather than sending him to the only school left open to him (which was in a different district),[91] his parents chose to continue his general education at home.

There was no shortage of unemployed Jewish professors able to undertake this task and who were only too pleased to be able to earn a little money. Erich's first tutor, Professor Deutsch, was arrested at the end of 1938 and was, with his wife, sent to a concentration camp. Erich was then taught by Professor Kaspar. This man was married to a Jewish woman and as a consequence had been suspended from his work, an illustration of why, perhaps, so many men divorced their Jewish wives.

It was recognised early on that Erich was gifted musically. His parents had bought a piano so that his older sister Ilse could learn, and he tinkered about on it and taught himself to play a Viennese waltz. His mum was so proud of him that she insisted he play it to Ilse's piano teacher, who was thrilled, and so before reaching his sixth birthday Erich started having piano lessons. He was initially taught by two lady teachers,[92] but at some point after the annexation tuition was taken over by Professor Leo Birkenfeld, who apparently was so strict that he almost robbed Erich of the pleasure of playing the piano. He was, however, a good teacher and Erich pays tribute to him for all that he taught him and

---

91 Leopoldstadt.
92 Mrs Klatovsky, followed by his uncle Ernst Waldmann's sister-in-law Mrs Steiner.

the encouragement which he gave Erich for his compositions. Sadly this came to an end in 1939 when the professor and his wife were arrested one night and eventually he finished up at Auschwitz.

They then found Professor Edmund Eysler, a well-known composer of the silver operetta era, as it was known. This Jewish man was married to a lovely Aryan wife, Leopoldine. As a result he and his children were partially privileged, though his music was not allowed to be performed. It was rumoured that the famous composer Franz Lehár had intervened on their behalf and they were allowed to stay in their own home throughout the war.

It was not until the war ended that Erich was able to attend the School of Music under Professor Alfred Uhl.

Ilse had wanted to study chemistry and was sad that she was prevented from going on to further education. She found a job as a secretary with a German industrial company called Flender and Co., dealing in steel and perhaps arms. Its offices were near the very grand Hotel Imperial. Needless to say, Ilse never disclosed that she had Jewish relatives and was able to keep this job throughout the Nazi era.

Anna's side of the family was not affected by the Nazi onslaught. Erich did not think that her parents were Nazis, but they did accept the advantages the annexation had brought. They nevertheless treated Robert with love and respect and were very kind to the children, and especially to Erich. Anna's dad died in 1939 and her mum in 1940.

Anna's surviving sister had married someone who, as Erich puts it, "swam along on the Nazi swell", and so contact with them became intermittent. In contrast, his Uncle Victor[93] was at least able to help the family financially. He had also bought a piano so that Erich could visit once or twice a week to give lessons to Aunt Anny, Victor's wife. Rumours started to circulate and, as everyone was afraid of being given away to the police, the visits had to stop. Erich gives them both credit for what they did for his family.

Despite the family's financial circumstances following Robert's bankruptcy, Anna had always managed to arrange a holiday during July and August. After the annexation she had explored various places to stay and eventually got a reply from Leopold Lothspieler, the local mayor at Ausser-

---

93 i.e. Anna's brother.

Ochsenbach in lower Austria and an SA man. Erich's mother decided to tell him the truth about the family. He said provided they were honest he would keep quiet about it, and of course he appreciated the extra money. Both he and his wife Josephine were very kind and Erich spent a lot of time there with his father, who was always treated with a lot of respect. Erich worked on their farm, ate with them in the farmhouse kitchen and was treated like a son. Sadly in 1941 when the Jewish star was introduced, these holidays had to end.

Bearing in mind what awful things happened under the Nazis, it is good to be able to note that there were at least some who showed some humanity. Erich still regrets that after the war in 1945 he did not check up on Leopold Lothspieler as presumably, having been a Nazi mayor, he would have been likely to have had a hard time. But there was just too much going on at the time and it was overlooked. This is not really surprising bearing in mind that Erich and his family had lost all their friends and the Jewish half of the family. Erich's father survived, as did my grandfather Bela who had emigrated. All the other siblings who had attended the festival gatherings in the past had lost their lives.

Erich remembers Kristallnacht on 9th November 1938. This was organised as a response to the murder of Ernst von Rath, a German diplomat in Paris. Erich watched as their synagogue in Neudeggergasse was burned, surrounded by a howling mob. With his generous nature he noted that there were some people who were dismayed and upset by it all.

Erich's mother was upset that despite her being an Aryan, the family had to give up their radio and valuables. The thing that sticks in Erich's mind was parting with a gold letter opener with a lovely woven handle.

In 1941 the family were forced to leave their flat at 8 Albertgasse, Josefstadt because it had been Aryanised. They moved to the second district, called Leopoldstadt, which had always been considered the Jewish quarter. The new address was a flat on the first floor at Franz-Hochedlinger-Gasse 23, which they shared with a very pleasant mixed-marriage couple, Arthur Fantl, who was Jewish, and his Aryan wife Mary.

Erich and his sister had to share a bedroom but it was large enough to take his piano too. They had managed to divide a largish living room to create a kitchen. They even had a bathtub connected to the drains, but the water had to be heated on the cooker. The Fantls seemed to have had the original bathroom; a small, windowless kitchen; and another room which presumably was their bed-sitting room. The toilet had to be shared and this was the only bone of contention, for when it got blocked, which was frequent, the other family was always to blame. Fortunately the couples got on well. They often sat and chatted in the living-kitchen and it was all very cosy.

Apart from another mixed-marriage couple in the flat above they had little contact with the other occupiers of the house, although they were not unfriendly. The exception was the concierge who lived below and whose illegitimate son was a Hitler Youth fanatic. She had been married to a Jew but divorced him, describing him as "a Jewish pig". He was deported to Theresienstadt. Not all the people who lived in the flats were Jewish or mixed-race couples, but the proportions are not known. Each flat in the house had a portion of the cellar assigned to it. This was to prove a very useful asset, as we shall see.

At about seventeen years of age[94] Erich was conscripted into a work unit of some thirty-five Jewish men. Some Jews did not have to wear a Jewish star,[95] but Erich was required to do so.

For around ten hours Monday to Friday and five hours on Saturday, Erich did heavy roadwork. There was a fifteen-minute break in the morning and forty-five minutes for lunch. Sunday was supposed to be a day off, but on many of these they had to work, transporting wood under the supervision of the SS. On these working Sundays they had to present themselves at 5am outside the Jewish cultural community centre in the Seitenstattengasse. (This is still the main synagogue and cultural centre in Vienna, and I think the only synagogue which was not destroyed during Kristallnacht.)

One day when they were in Vienna Woods, one-metre lengths of wood were being passed along by being thrown from one man to another. Erich, who was the last in the line, had to stack them on a lorry. Just as he was going to catch one, an SS man spoke to him and distracted him, with the result that his hand was squashed between the wood and the lorry, causing serious injury. He was off sick for a long time. The hand healed eventually but was damaged. He could still play piano, but the fluency on

---

94 Employed by Gusschebauer and Co. First date of work stated to be 16th April 1942.

95 Apparently Jewish partners of Aryans who had a child classed as a Class 1 mixed-race person.

his left hand had gone so that his ambition to be a piano virtuoso was at an end.

Erich was later employed in a garbage recycling depot for about five months, and then in 1943 when the bombs began to fall he was assigned to the roofers to repair or renew damaged roofs. During this time he was sent to Upper Austria for five weeks to renew an important road. He lived in a camp called Ebensee, which was under the direct jurisdiction of Mauthausen, a notorious concentration camp. The workers lived in wooden barracks surrounded by barbed wire and under SS supervision, being transported to and from the workplace by lorry. The SS regime was very strict but correct. They barked out their orders, but even in this situation there were some who showed some understanding of the fate of the Jewish workers and wanted to know more. Erich remembers one twenty-year-old named Gerdt Trost,[96] with whom he had a few satisfying conversations.

Things again changed in the autumn of 1944. Back in Vienna, Erich was handed over to the Vienna administrative district and joined a pioneer section of the German Army, who dealt with defusing detonators of unexploded bombs. He and the others with him had to dig out dead and entombed people and unearth any bombs which had not exploded but which were often deeply embedded. A pioneer, who was a German soldier, then defused them.

Again (and most interestingly), Erich found the relationship with the soldiers good as most were friendly and helpful. On one occasion he recalls a tragic incident. The bomb which they were working on was almost exposed and the leader of the pioneers, who was an expert at the job,[97] went down into the crater to defuse it. It was just routine. As it was almost lunchtime he called Erich over, gave him his ration card and asked him to get him two bread rolls from the grocer. Erich set off to do as he was asked and had hardly got round the corner when there was a loud explosion and it was all over for the pioneer and two of his comrades. Had he not asked Erich to get his lunch, he too would have been killed by the explosion.

It must have made the heavy and dangerous work easier to bear when the German soldiers they were working with were friendly, and Erich felt sorry that such a friendly man should have been killed.

---

96 He came from Minden/Westfalen (assumed Westphalia).
97 By name of Karl Grabner or something similar.

Working for the pioneers was better regulated and the working day was shorter. In addition, the workers were well fed by the German Army. That was fortunate as Erich and his father's ration cards were over-stamped with a 'J' and most of the pages were also over-stamped *invalid*, which meant that they got next to no food from these. In addition, there were restrictions as to where they could shop. Erich remembers that his meat ration was 150 grams[98] per week!

Fortunately for the family, Erich's mum was very industrious, working at weekends too to earn extra money. For hard cash it was possible to get everything on the black market. Her Czech employers were also very kind. They were anti-Nazi and knew the situation, so helped where they could with food and suchlike. Erich recalls that his first suit with long trousers was obtained through the good offices of Mr Rimesch, a colleague of his mother's.

Erich, too, was able sometimes to bring things home, including chocolate and cigarettes given to him by a pioneer. In addition, when he was working on the roof of the horsemeat market in Meidling, some meat became available now and then. Both his parents were heavy smokers, but Robert did not have a tobacco card as this was not permitted to Jews. He had to manage with fag ends and various teas and whatever Anna and Erich could bring home.

Erich has described wearing the Jewish star as singling him out, making him feel like a leper. It also could be dangerous as hooligans could have a field day with anyone who wore one.

Jews were not allowed to use the trams unless they could prove they were going to work, and then they had to ride on the outside platform.

Erich can remember vividly that on one occasion he had got onto a tram when one of the stolidly upright Viennese pulled him off the running board with the words, "Away with you, you Judas." To get over the situation Erich and his friends developed a technique of carrying a briefcase which they held in such a way as to obscure the view of the star. They had to be quick if challenged and drop it as the requirement was not merely to wear the star, but for it to be visible. Erich notes with amusement that even now when he carries a briefcase he will still hold it in the same position.

---

98   Erich has put *15dkgr*, which I have interpreted as 150 grams.

Another ploy was to obscure the star on their blue overalls by tacking a false pocket lightly over it. The plan was that if challenged they would quickly remove the tacked-on pocket and so reveal the star. What they had not considered was that, as the overalls became bleached with use, such a manoeuvre would have revealed a dark blue unbleached area which would certainly have led to questions. Fortunately he knows of no one who seemed to have been put to the test with this.

Not wearing the star was, of course, very dangerous. Erich initially stuck to the rules, but later wore it only sporadically, taking the risk of being caught even though he would have been subject to the severest of punishments. He also went to the cinema on many occasions, which was strictly forbidden, but again he was never caught. Looking back he can see what risks he was taking – but he was a teenager!

The absurdity of the Nazi rules can again be demonstrated by the rules applicable to Jews married to Aryans, which I have already alluded to. If they had children who were designated mixed-race Class 1, as was Ilse, then the Jewish parent did not have to wear the star. If the child was designated, like Erich, as a Jew, then they did. Similarly, if there were no children they had to wear the star. It follows that Erich's father was in an anomalous position as he had one child in each designation. He opted for the positive view and did not wear it.

Like most siblings, Erich and his sister argued and fought when young. She was the elder and so expected that he would do as he was told. Things changed for the better in their teenage years. Perhaps it was the terror of the times or the close proximity in which they had to live, but they understood each other well, discussed things and had no secrets from each other. Erich found her to be the best comrade ever and a great comfort to him. Both were very musical, she as a very good singer and he as a pianist and composer.

Bearing in mind the constraints of the times, it is surprising that they had either the wish or the ability to socialise. However, from 1943 theatrical evenings were held at the flat. Erich composed and Ilse performed his songs very well. She also wrote good texts herself and he composed the music for these, which she then was able to render beautifully.

Even more surprising is that sometimes thirty or so people were at these evenings, and they performed cabaret revues. Despite the war and the family's circumstances Erich remembers that his mum worked wonders, producing, as he put it, something out of nothing and making things cosy and comfortable.

He remembers some of the people who attended and maintained contact after the war. He appeared in various productions with Ernst Singer Walden, in particular one called *Musikalischen Programm* in Cabarett Dobner, for which Erich actually wrote the music. In later years, however, contact was lost with Ernst. On the other hand, Erich remains friends with Kurt Pollak to this day.[99] Kurt became a journalist and wrote theatrical pieces which were performed. They composed a number of songs (*Lieder*) together. Arminio Rothstein did well, becoming known as Clown Habakuk and having a successful career as magician and puppeteer after the war.

Remarkably, Erich has some photos which were taken in the flat. One of these shows a group of friends, including their flatmates the Fantls. Others are pictures of Erich at the piano and Ilse dressed up to sing. Even more remarkable is one which shows a band in the flat.[100] I presume they were able to get hold of a camera and film because of the position occupied by Erich's mum and perhaps sister.

Isle

99 March 2007.
100 In fact there were only three musicians: Ernst Fischl (violin), Armin Rothstein (drums) and Erich (piano). The other two were just holding instruments.

Erich (centre front) and friends

Erich and band

Viennese houses are very solidly built, but even so, with so many people in the flat and a band with drums playing, I wonder what the neighbours said. Erich says nothing about this.

Things changed on the 12th March 1945, the day the opera was bombed. Erich had been doing his demining job at Meidling. That day there were no trams running and as he walked home with his friend Kurt Pollak a terrible sight met them. The opera house was in flames! They continued homeward past the Stephen's Dom[101] and towards the river and Salztor Bridge. There Erich saw, to his horror, that searchlights were on despite the blackout and a search was going on in the next street to his. When he got home their house had also been hit and there was much damage, but not to his beloved piano. He was late home that day and his family had been worried, so one can imagine their joy on seeing that he was well.

A law at that time provided that if there was bomb damage one could stay at home for around ten days to repair what could be repaired. Erich's mum phoned the next day and sorted this out. Again it seems odd that, with all the oppression and ill treatment to which Jews were subjected, she was able to get Erich time off. Perhaps because he was working for the German Army at the time it was easier.

As cooking had become impossible, Anna also ensured that Erich and his father could go to the *Gulashcanon* (or public kitchen) with their dishes for a daily hot meal. Needless to say they kept their Jewish identity well hidden and presumably they were not asked to produce identity papers.

Towards the end of the period of work absence an ominous letter arrived with a call-up to the military command of the SS at the south-east rampart. It merely said that the Jew Erich was to present himself at a specified place and time with a suitcase holding clothes, blankets and eating utensils.

The family held a discussion and it was clear to all that the time had come for Erich to go 'underground'. Signs of disintegration were appearing and it was obvious to most people that the Russians were coming, so they hoped (as proved to be the case) that his disappearance would not be noticed. It was a very wise decision, for Erich later heard that those Jews who had heeded the summons and followed the order never returned and were probably done away with.

Being a 'U-boat'[102] was a very risky thing, for had Erich been found he would have suffered the same fate as some others who had been discovered in a street nearby and were shot on the spot.

The decision to go into hiding was taken on 20th March 1945. The family decided to utilise the cellar space which was allocated to them. Erich's mum, who was a most capable person, organised a bunk bed and Erich lay on the top section. Various suitcases, mattresses and boxes were

101 St. Stephan's Cathedral – see page 8
102 See page 177 re: U boats

piled up so as to make it appear as if it was merely a storage area. As a result, there was hardly any space to lie down. The cellar openings allowed light in and so he could just see to read in the daytime. His mum had organised a detector radio which enabled him to listen to music, but more importantly to the news which told of the advance of the Russians, all the time drawing nearer to Vienna. I do not know how on earth she did this as in 1938 they had been required to hand radios in as they were forbidden to Jews.

Anna came down to the cellar with some food and drink and to empty the necessary bucket, which was all that was available. It must have been a very difficult and stressful time for all of them.

As the Russians advanced the fighting got closer, and when it reached a town called Wiener Neustadt, the gunfire started. Everybody in the flat moved down to their tiny four-by-three-metre area of allocated cellar, six people in all. They brought down furniture, which in fact Erich still owns. As well as the bunk bed, there were two mattresses. Erich had to remain hidden on the top bunk as the authorities were checking all the time for deserters and refugees. Some of the Aryan flat-dwellers also moved down, presumably to their part of the cellar.

After the Russians had taken the first district of Vienna, the Danube Canal became the front line as the Germans were making a stand there. This lasted three days while the Russians were trying to take the crossing. There was heavy firing from rifles and machine guns.

The house next door was occupied by an SS command post. That was bad enough, but the SS men often came over to the cellar at night to chat and make speeches, but also no doubt because there were young and pretty girls there. Ilse had a friend who was a dancer and was staying with an aunt. The SS men brought wine, brandy and food and everyone, including Erich's parents and Ilse, pretended it was a pleasure to have them as visitors. Erich lay there hidden, listening to them bragging and cursing the Viennese, who had showered them with boiling water during their retreat through the Triester and Favoritenstrasse. They promised revenge when final victory was theirs. All the people in this small part of the cellar were of course terrified that a search might begin for Erich, but it never did. The strain of keeping entirely silent and still in a very confined space must have been awful.

The Russians found out that this SS command post existed and started targeting it. Erich's house received two hits. One of those went through the wall of the flat and damaged the piano, which, although subsequently repaired, was never the same again. The command post received a direct hit and collapsed down to the second storey.

The 13th April dawned. The silence was deathly. Erich's first thought was that the Nazis had won again and that the Russians had been driven back.

Just as he was thinking this, his mother rushed in and said, "Children, the Russians are here!" The horrific episode, the nightmare was over – they were free.

Erich rushed outside. The weather when he had gone into hiding had still been wintry. Now it was spring and the trees along the Danube were green. He and the rest of the family were grey, unkempt and unwashed. The situation outside apart from the weather was terrible too. Bodies, dead horses, rubbish, and a shot-up tank were scattered about.

Erich almost got shot by a Russian soldier who wanted his watch, which Erich had, with forethought, already hidden. At one point he saw a number of Russians knocking a young German soldier about, breaking his gun and shouting at him loudly. Erich felt an inexplicable compassion for this poor, trembling young man who only hours before had been the enemy.

Although much time has elapsed since those days, the scars of that period are still there and even now entering an official bureau such as a police station makes Erich's knees tremble.

After the war, Ilse married an actor. Erich did not get on with him and his relationship with Ilse was not restored until after the actor died. Sadly by then Ilse herself was very ill and died not long after her husband.

On a more cheerful note, Erich met his wife Gretl when he was playing the piano professionally at a spa hotel. A teacher by profession, she had been invited to stay and was tutoring the owner's children. Erich and Gretl married in 1953. They have two daughters, Susi Swartz, born on 18th June 1953, and Lisl Wieser, born on 10th February 1956.

After the war my parents must have been in touch with Erich and his family, and I can remember that when Mutti and I went to Vienna in 1979 we met with Erich and Suzi in a café in the Rotenturmstrasse. After our return home we completely lost touch. Well over twenty years later I found a piece of paper on which Mutti had written an address and telephone number for Erich. I tried it and so re-established the connection.

In 2004 I went to Vienna and met the family. It was then that Erich gave me a copy of his account of his experiences, which was of course in German. My sister Lisa translated it. After more enquiries of Erich, Lisa and I, with many contributions from my wife Wendy, did the initial rewrite and the above account is based on this.

23

Aunt Melanie Girkmann

Melanie Gertrude Steiner, born on 29th January 1903, was Aunt Edith's sister. Melanie married Karl Laurenz Girkmann on 25th September 1926. As Karl was a Roman Catholic the wedding took place in a registry office. However, Melanie was baptised into the Catholic faith on 31st March 1934, on which date the church also validated the marriage. The baptism and validation took place at St. Josef zu Margareten, 1050 Wien, Ramperstorffergasse 65.

Interestingly, my dad's sister Tante Martha got baptised in the same year. I think it is reasonable to assume that Tante Martha and Melanie knew each other, particularly as their married situations were not dissimilar. It is also reasonable to assume that they knew what was going on in Germany. Taking all the dates into account, I wonder if Melanie and Tante Martha were trying to pre-empt discrimination by being baptised. Whatever their motives, Melanie remained a Roman Catholic until her life's end and I think practised the religion.

Despite all this, when the Nazi annexation came Melanie and Karl decided to divorce. I assume that this was necessary so that he could keep his job. The divorce papers describe him as a *High School Professor in Engineering*, whereas Aunt Edith said he was a professor at the university and had published at least one book.

The couple applied for a divorce from table and bed (what we would call a legal separation) around 17th March 1938. As this was barely a week after the annexation they had probably already thought about it as it must have been known what was happening to Jews in Germany, and also that Hitler wanted to take over Austria.

Things then moved with remarkable speed. The reconciliation attempt, probably a statutory requirement, took place on 19th March and the hearing date was set for 29th March. On that date monthly maintenance was agreed. It was also agreed that the flat and most of the furniture belonged to Melanie.

Karl moved to I, Parkring, 4/2/2a. The Ringstrasse is one of the most prominent streets in Vienna. Melanie next appears in the records as a divorcee, and as having moved from the summer resort Voeslau on 19th September 1939 to an address in the third district in Gerlgasse, the home of Baroness Virginie Haas von Hagensfels. The baroness apparently told Melanie that provided she got her rent she did not want to know anything more about her, which was just as well.

Melanie spent the war years going to the flat of her 'ex-husband' and 'doing' for him. Although this meant travelling in Vienna she apparently was only recognised once, and that person did not betray her. Melanie's registration document confirms her occupation as a housekeeper and actually says it was *for husband*, though it seems that these words have been added in a different hand and so may be a later addition.

According to Aunt Edith, near the end of the war Melanie was summoned to present herself to the Gestapo. It was obvious that she took the summons seriously as I understand that she told her husband that she would have to go and that she might never come back. Aunt Edith says she was a good-looking woman and did not look Jewish. I expect she dressed herself up to the nines and presented herself with her papers. Happily she was not arrested and she survived.

Looking at the documentation which I have unearthed, another (and fascinating) reason becomes apparent, in addition to her appearance and gift of the gab, as to why she was able to escape the clutches of the Gestapo.

Melanie's parents were Philip Steiner and Helene Steiner, née Doerfler. However, in her registration documentation she says that her father was Franz Steiner, born on *28.12.70* (i.e. 1870) at Gainfarn, and that he died in Prerau. He is stated to be a Roman Catholic. She gives her mother's name as Marie Sikora, born on 21st August 1875 in Pressburg (Bratislava), also Roman Catholic, and stated as having died in Vienna. I have been unable to trace a registration document for Franz Steiner or Marie Steiner née Sikora, even though everyone was supposed to have one of these.

I then noted that when Karl filed his registration form he disclosed the name of his ex-wife Melanie but said he did not know the names of her parents. This is obviously ridiculous as they married in 1926, the marriage was validated in 1934 after her baptism, and I have been informed that the baptismal record correctly records her parents' names. There seem only two possible explanations for this omission. Either Karl did not want to name them to try to protect Melanie or, more likely, he did not know the false names which Melanie was using to hide her identity. It is rather surprising that his registration documents were accepted with these omissions.

The inevitable conclusion to be drawn from this is that Melanie had assumed a false identity and been provided with forged papers. It is, I suppose, quite possible that the Roman Catholic church was involved in some way (especially as Melanie was a baptised member), but not surprisingly I have not been able to find any records. It would have been great if I had been able to have a sight of any personal papers after she died as this might have clinched the argument.

Looking at the documentation now I can see some weaknesses which could have exposed them to risk. For example, Karl's omission mentioned above. Also that Marie Sikora is stated to have died in Vienna, so it would have been a relatively easy matter to check the death records. If she was a fictitious person this would quickly have become apparent. It may however be that because of the war not all deaths were properly recorded. It is also possible that for whatever reason the Gestapo were disinclined to follow up leads or make further enquiries.

When the war ended the need for subterfuge disappeared and Karl and Melanie were again able to live together as husband and wife. They lived on the Parkring, but at a different address. Karl died first and is buried in the cemetery in Simmering. The gravestone says he died in 1959, but strangely the burial record says the burial took place on 22nd November 1961, which is odd to say the least.

Melanie continued to live at the same address. I have a vague recollection of visiting her with Mutti, and that I thought she was a rather formidable lady. On 20th January 1969 Melanie died in the Sophie Hospital, principally of arteriosclerosis. She is buried with her husband in the grave at Simmering.[103]

---

103 Grave reference: Part A, Group15, Row 1, Number 9.

24

Chava Livni, Née Fuerst

Chava Livni – on left

Strictly speaking Chava's story should not be included here as she is not really a relative of mine. She is related to Erica, the daughter of Gustav Waldmann, whose wife was the cousin of Chava's mother. Gustav was one of the brothers of my grandfather, and so my great-uncle.

However, Chava's story is so poignant and interesting that I will claim her through Erica.

What is written here is based on the account which Chava herself wrote. Some of that document was addressed to her father, even though she knew at the time of writing that he had perished.

Born on 21st July 1926, Chava was brought up in Bratislava in Slovakia. The country was not initially occupied by the Germans. This came in 1944, but there was a fascist puppet government in place from 14th March 1939 and Jews were persecuted under that government's rule.

As had been the case in Austria prior to the annexation in March 1938, life for Chava and her family had been good and they were able to live comfortably. Chava can remember going out for walks with 'Fraulein' the nanny. Life was normal; she played with her cousin Liese Fleischhacker, read books, and went to a Protestant school where she had a beloved teacher, Edith. She and her friends walked around the old town or visited places in the vicinity, often in the company of her father. It all seemed so secure, as if it would last forever.

Things changed when she was attending the German high school, where at that time almost half the children were Jewish. That was until one day when a group of Hitler Youths stood outside and turned all the Jewish children away. Chava was then sent to a Slovak school, but as she did not speak the language she was very unhappy. This was followed by a year in a Jewish school, but by the time she was fourteen schooling came to an end for her.

Her family were not religious and held humanistic beliefs. They did not regard either nationality or religion as important. The only thing that mattered to them was whether a person was a good human being. Chava never knew until the Jewish laws were introduced who of the family friends were Jews. It was not important.

As more and more anti-Jewish laws were introduced, her father lost his job at the bank and of course had to wear the Jewish star, as did they all. They had to hand over their valuables, just the same as if they were living under direct Nazi rule. They were restricted from going to public parks, cinemas and theatres, but despite these restrictions the young people managed to enjoy themselves. They used to meet in the cemetery, taught themselves in small groups, invented a card filing system which they called *registka* for recording historical and geographical facts, discussed books and had long debates.

When she was about twelve or thirteen Chava joined a Zionist Youth movement and this became her 'second home'. Her parents did not approve as they still held to their humanistic beliefs.

In 1939 three of her mother's brothers and their families decided to be baptised as they hoped it would help their situation. They tried to persuade Chava's family to do the same, but her father decided to discuss it with Chava first as he said that at thirteen she was old enough to make up her own mind. Chava thought about it and decided against it. Later she learned that her father had taken the same decision. In the event, it would have made no difference to their treatment whether they had been baptised or not.

As happened to Jews in in Austria, the family were forced to leave their flat, which was deemed too large for them, and went to live with Chava's grandmother, whose flat was also considered too large for a single person.

Chava obviously enjoyed the Zionist Youth movement. Groups were formed for training mainly in agriculture, and they worked first in a vineyard, and then in a large vegetable garden which had belonged to one of her uncles.

A few of the groups in the movement decided they wanted to live together as a commune, and train together and then go to Palestine. Chava's group went to Čadca, a small town near the Polish border, but initially she was not allowed to join them. It took several weeks before she could persuade her parents to let her go, and she eventually went in 1941.

Her time at Čadca is blurred, but she remembers hard work, intense living, learning Hebrew, friendship and talks into the night. And in particular there was Motke, the youth leader, who was adored by all. Families sent packages from home which were shared, and after the work there was singing and music... And then it suddenly ended.

Rumours about transports to the East proved to be true. Everybody over the age of sixteen had to go. Chava was one of three girls who were sent home because they were too young. There were also a few boys and girls who happened to be away on the day and so were spared the transport. Chava found it so sad to have to part from the rest of the movement, with no idea what the future held for the others, but the worst they imagined was that there would be hard work and perhaps hunger. It was only months later that she learned that her friends had died in Treblinka, which was an extermination camp.

After Chava had returned from Čadca she kept a diary for a time, and also wrote a number of letters which in fact were never sent. She left these with her friend Aviva, who managed to save most of them. I am going to quote some of them below. They reveal what terrible times they were, confusion regarding what had happened to her friends, and how much pain and anguish Chava felt.

April 12th 1942
Motke is no more, is no more forever! Such strange words, what do they mean? Motke went away… Never again… One after the other went… It is happening so fast – how to bear it? How to bear the "never again"? How to be strong, how not to break apart? I feel as if all of you were dead – just I am still here – can it be true?

May 27th 1943
Now I know what it means to be a Jew! Now I live it with all the pain and suffering.

June 6th 1942
Now Shuli went too – day before yesterday they took her. It is strange – there is no more pain, perhaps I cannot feel any more? I am just numb and tired… Cars, cars with people. Wagons crammed with people…

June 7th 1942
3 days of transports. We work, make packages, hundreds of packages – hands move all the time, all the time the same rhythm – just don't think! One-two one-two – close the package put it on the side – the next one. But the pain is with me all the time and all of you who went away – your eyes… so many eyes…

June 10th 1942
Motke we can write to you. Oh God, I am so glad! But what can a written word on a small piece of paper say? But if you get it, you will know that we think of you all the time – please, please be strong! Perhaps one day we shall meet again?

June 11th 1942
We have some news of where our boys and Motke are. We try to write – and hope that they get it…

July 7th 1942
No, I cannot imagine this – not Motke! That they shoot you and pour lime on you??! No, no no!!!

July 20th 1942
Tomorrow I will be 16. Such a strange feeling – so different from every other birthday. Till this moment I did not even remember – now I am just sad. Will I live on my 17th birthday?… Everything is so grey – Motke and you all – be strong, be hard like stone – just deep, deep inside leave a bit of feeling!

August 6th 1942
There is again a possibility of aliyah[104] it seems like a fata morgana.[105] And to think of you all ("you go on aliyah and us they shoot in the Ukraine") – that is so hard. It is even hard to know, that we continue living here – everyday lives day after day.

August 22nd 1942
(This is a very unusual entry as it recounts a dream, which will be referred to later.)
Motke, yesterday I was with you – just for a while. I thought so much of you and then I saw you – lying on a cot in a hut – and you looked at me and I thought: "do you know that it is Friday evening? Do you remember us too?…"

September 22nd 1942
Motke – today half a year ago you wrote to us – after they took the boys. I still see you in my mind on the last day in Čadca – you stood in the door and looked after us, so sad… When will there be an end to the waiting?

November 11th 1942
I dreamed: all of us sat round a long table and somebody distributed apples.

---

104 Means a possibility of emigrating to Palestine.
105 Another way of saying 'mirage'.

Beautiful red apples. But there were not enough for everybody – so whoever got one, had to share. But nobody did. I got an apple too and started to cut it to pieces – I cut and cut – the apple did not diminish every time I gave a piece away there was a new piece…

December 17th 1942
Motke, I have to know if you are alive! It is awful not to know where to send my thoughts – and all the news we get… I tried to think of the thousands who die – what right have I to be anxious about individuals? But can one stop it? There are no words – there is no help I cannot write any more – there is no sense in it. I cannot hope any more – I just wait and wait and am afraid of the day when there will be nothing to wait for any more. Such emptiness…

January 25th 1943
Motke again they speak about aliyah. This time it seems a real possibility – but how can I leave? How can I bear to be so far away? Do you remember – once you said, that after many many years we will meet an old man with a long beard on the road – and we will be young… The thought that you could come back and not one of your "children" waits for you.

March 21st 1943
Motke – I read your last letter again, for the thousandth time – how is it possible that a year has passed? And no one knows if one of the boys lives…

December 12th 1943
I have not written for a long time – I just did not have the strength for it. These last days I sat with Hayka and translated her diary and lived through it all: how her group hid in the ghetto and finally managed to escape.
Today I know that my friends who went with a transport are not alive any more. In the long hours at night, when I cannot sleep I just ask: "how???" How much did you suffer – what unspeakable tortures you had to suffer?
Is it possible, that there are places in this world where people live normal lives? How can they? And if I should survive – how can I ever live a normal life? Of one thing I am sure – as long as I live I will not forget!

(This is the last entry in the diary.)

Despite all the persecution that went on, there was organisation within the Jewish community in the form of a Jewish Council, of which Chava's father was the head of finance. At some time prior to her return from Čadca, and within the umbrella of the Jewish Council, an underground 'Working Group' was formed, to which her father also belonged. It was set up to try to salvage what could be saved. The soul of this group was Gisi Fleischmann, an ardent Zionist (who as it happens was also the person instrumental in persuading Chava's parents to let her go to Čadca). The group was a mixed bunch, with assimilated Jews like Chava's father, and two rabbis, one Orthodox; the other Reformed.

Even so, Gisi, using a motto, "The good of the community goes before personal interests", managed to get cooperation.

It became apparent that the most urgent activity was to try to save people. Some members of the youth movement group went illegally over the border to Hungary, where the situation was better at the time. Those who stayed behind started to manufacture false papers and gave them to those who did not look too Jewish. They also tried to find hiding places for others.

Even with false papers it was not easy to live as an Aryan as one had to have food ration cards. Chava records that despite the danger they found people who helped. There was a policeman who supplied ration cards and sometimes even bread. There was a washerwoman, Katica, who rented out rooms to workers and was willing to take people without papers for a few days. Her home was the first haven for many who fled from Poland.

Chava herself and her friend Aviva found work as babysitters with Jewish families, which of course included daily hand-laundry for the babies. They managed to earn some money that way, so that they could send food parcels to friends in work camps.

Chava and her family had a narrow escape during this time as they were taken to a concentration point at the town hall, to be sent on a transport. However, they were let out at the last moment as her father was the head of finance. At that time they were living with the Fleischhacker family. When they were rounded up Chava's aunt had boiled all the eggs in the house so that they then had to live on hard-boiled eggs for days afterwards.

The transports, one of which had taken Chava's friends away to Treblinka, stopped in autumn 1942. No one knew for how long, but each day was a gift.

Aviva (left), Chava(middle), Sonja (right)

They had to move again. Her grandmother went to a place called Nitra where a relative was working as a doctor, and he took her into hospital as a patient. The rest of them, including the Fleischhacker family, moved into a flat on the bank of the Danube. Normally they would not, as Jews, have been allowed to live there, but Chava's uncle had an 'exception' as he had gone to school with the Catholic priest Tiso, who was the head of the Slovak Autonomous Republic. Even so, as Jews they had to be home by six in the evening, but they amused themselves by looking at the vessels on the Danube. Chava remembers envying the children living with their families on the barges.

Chava was still in the youth movement. They could not meet in groups of more than three, so one person in each group was always a member of another group so that they could communicate. The two others in Chava's group were Aviva and Sonja.

They socialised, mainly in the kitchen, listening over and over again to a few records they possessed, played on an old hand-operated phonograph.

Time passed and her memories of this period are hazy, but Chava remembers travelling to the end of the tram line on separate trams and then meeting up with others for a few hours. She remembers trying to teach Yiddish and translating a diary for Hayka, a girl who had escaped with a group from a ghetto in Poland. The diary is referred to in one of the quotes above.

The movement was still engaged in finding hiding places for refugees from Poland, and tried to find ways of sending them on to Hungary.

On one occasion Chava and Aviva were in the old town and someone spoke to them through a barred window. It turned out that the house was a prison and the prisoner an arrested Jewish communist. They took him some food, and when he was transferred to another prison they took parcels there too.

Mariska, a Christian girl, was a good friend who went to Hungary several times, taking money and contacting friends.

Chava notes that some of the Jewish people joined the partisans, but even that was not easy as they were not very friendly towards Jews either.

Nineteen forty-four was a momentous year. In the spring two escapees from Auschwitz came back with exact information about the gas chambers and crematoria. There had been suspicion and a sense of doom before, but it was a shock to hear the details of the planning and the scope of the annihilation. It was also now clear that no one who was on a transport would be seen again.

In the summer of 1944 the partisans organised an uprising. The uprising precipitated the German occupation, and with that the renewed danger of transports. There were feverish attempts to avoid this danger. Cousin Liese and her parents had already moved out of the flat by the Danube and gone to stay with a married sister elsewhere. Chava and her family went to a village and hid in the cellar of a house that belonged to a neighbour's maid. How long they stayed, she cannot remember. They only came out of the cellar late at night for a breath of fresh air.

Then one day her father got news that there were negotiations with the Germans and that the danger had passed. He wanted to take part in the negotiations, and as the family did not want to be separated they all returned with him. A fatal decision, for it was on that very night that the Germans came for them.

The date was 29th September 1944. Chava writes movingly:

This is the end… it is night, we stand beside the Danube, a few people guarded by Hlinka[106] guards. Silence – the water is black, only the moon shines silver on the water. This is the moment of leave taking – I am 18 years old and say good-bye to life, because I know: this is the end. I would like to scream, to resist – but it is hopeless.

---

106 The ruling political party was known as the Hlinka Party and it armed units as the Hlinka Guard.

Chava and the others were marched to the offices of the Jewish Council, where they waited and spent the night. She cried softly as she felt her life was about to end before it had even begun, but she tried to be strong and said to herself that others had gone before and she would bear it too.

When morning came any thoughts of escape could not be entertained as the chance of doing so was hopeless, and besides, even if she could, Chava would not leave her parents as they needed her help. That morning they were put on a train and initially taken to a camp at Sered,[107] where there was chaos and shouting. Chava thinks they were there only for a few days.

They were again herded into a cattle wagon. Conditions were terrible. There was hardly any room to sit. Chava felt disorientated, as if she were not really there and looking in on the scene. Across from her in the wagon there was a couple with children and Chava cuddled one, an eight-year-old called Mindel, and asked herself, Why should this child die? She looked at the parents and thought, They will never have grandchildren, and I will not have a child of my own. It was best not to think. The train moved on; it does not matter where, because it led to death.

While she was in the wagon in such a hopeless situation, Chava felt a strong, warm hand holding hers. She could not see his face, nor did she know his name, and could only hear his voice and feel the kindness and caress of his hand. He talked to her quietly. Within herself, she felt at peace. She felt the terror around her but wanted to dream and forget it – to dream of happiness. Despite the crowds it was as if they were all alone and they were able to talk about everything, including the death that awaited them. He kissed her eyes and mouth and she kissed him too – the next day they did not expect to be alive, and they just had those few moments.

Eventually they arrived at their destination. Chava describes it in her own words:[108]

---

107 It is not relevant to the story, but Sered was the birthplace of my maternal grandmother.

108 This was recorded by Chava following liberation of Mauthausen in1945.

And then we arrive – they open the carriages, shouting, beating and the order: men on this side! I cannot talk – I stand between him and my father, hold their hands… one more moment… my parents kiss, they are so strong! And he kisses me for the last time – promise to be strong! My father hugs me – somebody pulls me away – just his words stay with me "I lived my life – but you had everything still in the future…"

I cannot speak, I cannot cry. I have to be strong – for my mother, for Agi[109]… The voice asks: "able to work? Go on." A hand pushes us on – mother where are you? We are not allowed to stop, to look back – we only hear her crying in despair: "My children, my children!" – If I would get to be 100 years old I will not forget…
Go on, keep it all inside – deep, deep inside. Be hard as a stone, just a little while longer and then you won't be anymore! The night is dark only the strong lights of the searchlights pierce the fog and blind… Barbed wire fences, mud, huts – unreal forms of people in striped prisoners garb – Auschwitz! So that is how it looks!

A long line of trucks – we cannot see into them. Shouts "to the side" – I do not know what the cars mean – just an idea – Then the showers: I am sure, this is the end. We have to strip off all clothes – I hold Agi's hand. A photo fell out of a pocket – Avi, Puffi and I sitting on a bench and laughing. I hurt so much – be well, all my loved ones – for me there is nothing more.

They cut our hair – I sit naked and my hair on my knees. The girl that goes now with a razor over my head is here since 1942 – she knew Mela and tells me about her death… I am numb, can't take in anything more. The shower – and what comes out is water – not gas!!! We live! We get some rags, wooden clogs – it does not matter. Agi found a kerchief in a pocket, goes to return it "hide it, you goose". They herd us into a hut – people lying crowded together on cots – like sardines. The light is shut off – in the dark we climb somewhere, try to lie down, half-sitting – somebody lies across my legs – never mind. We keep holding hands – only to stay together – and close the eyes and forget…

Coarse shouts wake us: "roll call, roll call – everybody out!" These are Jewish

---

109 Agi was Chava's only sister. She was about two years younger and also survived.

girls shouting at us – in good warm clothes, boots and beating us with clubs. They beat us – "faster, faster!" – I don't get it – I knew so much about Auschwitz – but that our girls can behave like this...

It is still dark, only a red glow in the sky. It is 4 o'clock in the morning, cold and rainy. The block-elder counts us like merchandise – after her trail the "Stubovky". What is this smell? Impossible to define: lime, corpses, fire – Auschwitz.

We stand for hours – finally the order to disperse. The whole body is stiff, aches – but never mind! Only stop thinking – don't think!! Back to the hut – now in the daylight I see it: the bunks, the long brick stove in the center – I have seen this before, I know this – it is my dream! The dream where I saw Motke! How is that possible?

We huddle in the bunks – slowly we recognize people – without hair they look different. Agi cries and cries – I try to quiet her down – empty words... I myself don't believe them! People talk, try to orient themselves, to find a glimmer of hope – to ignore the hopelessness, the bleakness... We get soup – an unspeakable brew full of twigs and stones. But I force myself and Agi to eat it – I know that is the only way to stay alive.

A terrible scene: suddenly a woman falls on her knees in front of me and thanks me for having saved her daughter. I had brought her false "Aryan" papers -"you saved her and did not manage to save yourself!"
Somebody from the men's camp is looking for me – some kind of workman, they can get around the various camps. News from father – I dare not believe. Can he stand it? Is there a little bit of hope that we shall meet again?? If I could pray, I would pray for strength – for him, for me...

The fifth day in Auschwitz. Evening, it is already dark – suddenly: detonations. Again and again – now we are sure – it is anti-aircraft cannon! Shouts from outside: "Put the lights out!" – on and on, like an echo. Perhaps there is after all a small possibility to survive – not to go to our death? We hold hands – we hope – there is no fear. What have we to lose? – Then a morning, like every other morning here. Nothing happened. Again "coffee" (a brown tasteless watery brew) and be counted and the horrible latrines and the soup… The "Musel-women", hardly able to put one foot before the other, looking like skeletons. Auschwitz! And always the smoke stacks – smoking and the red glow… And then curfew – Agi almost faints – I half-carry her to the door, there maybe some fresh air will enter through a crack. Roll call again – standing around – disinfection – we receive summer clothes and out we go into the ice-cold night and pouring rain – finally we end up in a hut. No light, no blankets, just shouts and beatings, nobody knows what is going on. We are not allowed to leave the room, at last a pail is brought into the midst of the hut and 1000 women may relieve themselves, one after the other. It is horrible, but they cannot demean me. As long as I am alive nothing can humiliate me – what there is deep inside me stays with me, whatever they do to me!

Next day again: all out! Without clothes we stand in the rain for hours. Now I am sure, this is the "selection", after that there is only the gas… I am glad – at last the torture comes to an end.

Once more the thoughts go out to all those I am not going to ever see again – my mother who has all this behind her. My father – maybe there is a miracle and he survives? And all the friends. We had planned our future together…

Laboriously we trudge along in the too large wooden clogs – again the showers – again – no gas! Again the girls from 1942 distribute clothes. We stand until the evening – but now it seems to be sure – they send us with a workers transport. That I also did not know – that there is an "After" after Auschwitz… At last we move – a long line, parting at a van. Again the fear – just now we had some hope and now? But it is only the distribution of some food.

And again in the train wagon – again people piled on each other – but we two stayed together… Slowly I start to think again, to hope – it is hard to grasp. We are alive and we again dare to hope…

The journey from Auschwitz took Chava to Freiberg in Eastern Germany. This time they were housed in a factory hall which, hard to believe, was heated, and there were washrooms! One could almost feel human again.

The group that came from Auschwitz had a camp elder called Hanka and a room elder called Sari. These two were sisters, and both had travelled with them from Auschwitz.

The elders were privileged with regard to both food and accommodation. There were perhaps 1,500 women brought from Auschwitz, some of them originally from Vienna and other places, via Theresienstadt. Those from Poland had their own elder organisation. The women were guarded by female SS guards and the camp was under an SS camp commandant.

Chava was allocated to work in an aircraft factory and assigned to the wing department, supervised by German foremen who spoke with a Saxonian dialect which she could barely understand. The work initially involved filing and rasping aluminium sheets, and was done standing up.

The days now consisted of roll call in the morning, 'coffee', then work, midday 'soup', more work, another roll call, and then an evening ration of bread with a bit of jam, or sometimes even something that resembled a sausage, awaited them on their beds. When they first arrived at Freiberg they occasionally had some boiled potatoes too.

Luxury accommodation it was not. They were very crowded: two to a narrow cot full of bedbugs, but at least it was warm. At times they could wash, but there was no soap.

Chava records: *We are dead tired from the long hours of work, but still in the evenings we are again human beings.* Perhaps someone would recite a poem or talk of what it was like before, or fantasise about what it would be like 'afterwards', which usually meant eating a thick slice of bread and butter. Sometimes they sang sad sentimental songs, and there were tears.

During the evenings a young SS woman used to come in and sit in a corner quietly. "Please don't mind me," she used to say, and while she sat there she cried her heart out. One day they heard that she had been punished and removed from the camp.

Chava does not say why the woman cried or whether anyone tried to find out. It may be that she was just depressed or worried about her family, but it would be nicer to think that perhaps her heart was moved by the plight of the women in whose room she sat.

Hanka, the elder, and her sister had more commodious accommodation. Someone found out that Chava had taken part in séances. She and the others involved were taken into the elders' room to teach them, and thus Chava got some measure of protection. It was for a short time a luxury not to be in the crowded room, and to get an additional potato or two, or the kettle with the dregs of the soup which she could then share with the others in their room.

Work was endless, but during the drilling and polishing of the parts there was time to think; if anything, too much time. Thoughts of home and who, if anyone, had survived.

Christmas Eve 1944 came. They had a bonus and were allowed to 'buy' some celery salt, for which they received some kind of ration card that was not valid for anything else.

This also proved to be the end of 'the good time', as they were to discover. They had to move out into huts which had been built for them outside the town. The women were initially taken into an open shed during a snowstorm and had to fill straw mattresses to sleep on. The cold was biting. Chava remembers that through her thin shoes with their soles almost gone, her feet felt like blocks of ice. Her fingers could scarcely move – the cold, if anything, was even worse than the hunger – but somehow she filled the mattress. The pain she experienced when she went back into the warm factory as her feet and hands thawed out was even worse, and not surprisingly despair crept back as she wondered how she could go on.

They now had to walk to and from work through the town. In the morning, still in total darkness with hardly anyone on the streets except for a line of freezing women, some holding small children, waiting for milk. Back again in the dark to the huts, which did have stoves but they were not lit.

The vast expanse of snow looked dreadful to Chava. The only thing that gave her some hope was seeing a barren tree, windswept on a hillock, withstanding the storm, and the thought that when spring came it would be green again.

At one point Chava was ordered to polish wings with a huge polishing disc, which cost her her last remaining reserves of strength. She said she was fortunate: the foreman was humane and she was sent back to her old job. The foreman there was quite nice too. At Christmas he had hidden a bag with sweets between the ribs of the wing for them to find, and on another occasion some bandaging for their feet, which were wounded and not healing. He too had worries, for he told them he had not heard from his family who lived in Düsseldorf, and that there had been many aerial attacks.

There were air raids at Freiberg too. When the alarm sounded everyone hurried to the shelters, except the prisoners who were left locked in the factory. Nevertheless, each bomb blast sounded like a present to them. Chava remembers seeing the bombs falling on Dresden[110] with the flames painting the sky and illuminating the destruction. One of the SS guards was distraught as her family lived there, but for the prisoners it meant that the end was getting nearer.

Occasionally one of the women had to go to the electrician's shop to get a replacement light bulb. There were Frenchmen working there who had built a radio, and from them they got some news about the front line.

Even though it must have been clear that the war was lost, it did not diminish the zeal of the guards. One of the girls was caught by a guard for some crime or other and her best friend was made to shave off her hair. It grows back very slowly, particularly if you are starved, perhaps two centimetres in three months, but even that is better than being bald.

As time progressed, food rations got smaller. There was less bread and thinner turnip soup. Soon the only thing Chava and the rest of them could think about was food. They told each other stories of wonderful meals, but really all they wanted was bread, and enough of it.

Chava said she was never vain, but when she caught a glimpse of herself in a windowpane she could not believe how she looked. Dead eyes looked back with hollow cheeks, a skeleton covered with rags. It must have been very difficult, but she tried to hold on and refused to see herself as a *Muselmann*.[111] Neither she nor the other women menstruated, which as she said was just as well, but it did make her wonder about her womanhood and whether, if she survived, she would be able to have children. However, she had to be realistic and realised that despite her will to live, the chances were that she and the others would be liquidated or 'go up the smokestack' as the saying went.

As conditions worsened the behaviour of the prisoners deteriorated and became more animal-like. Chava remembers a mother and daughter quarrelling over a piece of bread. The cohesion among the prisoners diminished. The room elders remained well fed and clothed. Those of the prisoners who were in outside working groups received additional food

---

110 February 1945, from Wikipedia.
111 A term used for walking skeletons in concentration camps who had given up the will to live.

rations and so still looked like human beings, and this made them look down on the others who were worse off than they – as if they were from another race.

But there were exceptions to this behaviour too. Chava remembers Mrs Neumann, who encouraged the young ones by telling them not to let it get them down. There was Mrs Mela from Vienna who never lost her sense of humour, and there were others who supported each other and helped. And there was Inge, an older woman and a close friend. Her condition was particularly tragic. She was half-Jewish and had been married to a Gentile. When he was killed on the Eastern Front she, together with her Jewish grandmother, was sent to Theresienstadt where she worked as a nurse and then remarried. Shortly after that her second husband was sent to the East and, like many other women at Theresienstadt, she volunteered to accompany him. Chava said they were just so innocent!

Chava was determined to keep her human dignity. Nothing, she said was going to demean her – the shouting or the cursing, or the slap in the face for asking for a pair of shoes.

The days dragged on, marching to and from the factory, getting to know the route in detail, aware of the corner where the wind was especially biting and the funny scene when the SS commander hurrying them along tried to show them how to get rid of lumps of snow from their shoes and fell over on his bottom. No one dared to laugh. The factory had one advantage: it was warm (once, I suppose, one had got over the pain of thawing out).

It was now Easter, and it was spring. They had a day off and sat in the sun in the yard. They washed their ragged clothes and themselves, and even here they were insulted with expressions like, "You swine again in the bathroom."

But there was something else. A short time before an elderly SS woman had been retired, it was rumoured she had been considered too humane.

Now she walked by on the outside of the fence and, without stopping, said, "Just a little bit more patience – the front line is already very near!"

Domestically within the huts, things were happening too. The Polish elder had a baby and the SS commander seemed to be very decent about it and got her some milk. Could this be a sign of the end coming, Chava wondered? One of the Slovak girls in the camp was also pregnant. She had managed to hide it till the last moment, but now it was evident. The women had been in the early stages of their pregnancies when sent to Auschwitz and passed the 'selection' without anyone noticing. Had their condition been known, they would have been gassed.

It was obvious that things were going from bad to worse for the Germans. Chava could see long lines of refugees trudging along. They too looked wretched, and one could not feel good about it even if it was the 'master race' looking like this.

The factory stopped working and they were confined to camp. They could hear artillery in the distance. How long would it be before they were liberated? During this wait the Slovak baby was born and named Hanka after the camp elder.

And then for Chava another roll call, and off to the railway station and back into the wagons, this time open ones. The same scenes of overcrowding, stench, no place to relieve oneself, increasing hunger and terrible thirst and diarrhoea. Overarching it all was the thought, *Will the next stop be the gas chamber?* To have been so close to liberation and then to be moved on must have been unbearable. The train meandered along, stopping and starting. Other trains were seen, one from Buchenwald, on parallel tracks. On one occasion they were allowed off the train when rags from another train were thrown out. They were told these items came from people who had typhoid, but they did not care and each chose something for themselves.

They were without food for days until one day the camp commander managed to get some sugar for them. On another occasion people on a bridge threw bread into the wagons. While stationary in a small Czech village, a delegation of local citizens asked permission to provide food. This was granted and they turned up with huge kettles and baskets.

Chava remembers sitting there with a cup of coffee with milk and a piece of white bread. She asked rhetorically, "Does that still exist?" After all the hardship and privations she now found herself crying, unable to stop, as if those items were greetings from another world which had once existed.

A long line of exhausted, skeletal women arrived at Mauthausen, a notorious concentration camp which was located in Austria. They had to walk up a steep hill and Chava felt she could not go on, but knew that to drop behind would be fatal. One of the girls, named Trude, whimpered, but they pulled her along with them.

At last they were in the camp and were given some food; then out into the yard. It was raining and night-time, but they did not care. They had to wait for their shower. Would this be gas or water? Once more it was water, and warm water at that, which made them feel weak but human. They were handed clothes of sorts – torn men's underpants and shirts.[112]

Two days later they were moved again to the so-called 'gypsy camp' at what was known as the Vienna Ditch. (This was a quarry; a three hundred-foot crevice separated from the main camp by 186 steps and a jagged cliff. It was a place where great cruelty had been carried out by the SS.)[113] Chava describes the camp as horrible, with almost no food and a bit of straw on the floor to sleep on.

They were housed in an enormous barrack containing hundreds of women. Although they were all, in a sense, in the same boat there were groupings among the prisoners. In one corner were the Ukrainian women, who were fighting each other like animals. Opposite Chava's group were 'antisocial' Germans, namely prostitutes who, Chava said, despite the presence of all the other women there, continued to practise their profession with German soldiers who had free access to the barracks. Things must have been pretty bad, for one of Chava's neighbours told her to cover her sister with a blanket so that she would not be able to see. Except for Trude, they had been separated from all the others that they knew.

And then, from an unexpected source, Chava received a gift. One of the prostitutes gave them a book by Cronin. It was a real book, and in the heart of the inferno in which they found themselves, surrounded by ear-splitting shouts, shrieks and quarrels, they were able to escape into another world.

At night the guns could be heard. They did not know where the front line was, but hoped that this time they would not be sent on.

And then came a morning when there were no SS guards, and also no food. At first they could not grasp what this could mean and were too weak and empty to feel any happiness. For all the months that had passed Chava had held out for this moment, and now she could not feel a thing.

---

112 Chava has told me that the gas chambers stopped working the day before they arrived.

113 Information from an article by Ray Jones at www.spectacle.org/496/camps. html

After a while they plucked up courage to leave the barracks. They could not believe their eyes, for a white flag was flying at the main camp!

Once this was realised, all hell broke loose in the barracks. The Ukrainian women were apparently almost killing each other. Chava and Agi decided on the spur of the moment to go to the main camp. They took Trude with them, but she had no shoes. Agi managed to pick up a pair from near where the Ukrainians where fighting.

They walked down the road and nobody tried to stop them. There was shooting overhead but they just continued to walk. They were free and could not be hurt any more – all they had to do was to get away. They stopped at a farmhouse and asked for food, and were given a slice of bread with lard and sausage. What bliss it was to bite into such a thick piece of bread!

It was now 7th May 1945.[114] It was impossible for Chava to grasp that just a few days before she and the rest were near to death without expectation of freedom, and now they were free. As they reached the men's camp the front line had already moved on and the Americans had left the camp in the hands of the Underground, which was well organised there.

Not much time was wasted by the Underground, who immediately mobilised Chava and the rest to search the SS barracks for munitions. As they sat in one of these barracks someone cooked soup and they talked to the young boys, most of whom came from Poland. They were total strangers, but they talked as if they had known each other forever.

By 8th May (which incidentally is Victory in Europe Day) things were already improving, for Chava recounts that they had 'decorated' their room and had curtains and a tablecloth. She was able to shower with hot water, and had soap. Getting rid of the filth was wonderful, and they also had clean clothes at last, even if they were SS uniforms. There was also a stove that worked, and a French cook who, oddly, warned them against eating the American food, which was mainly bacon and beans. He instead toasted slices of potato for them on the stove. He also managed to obtain opium which was used to stop diarrhoea.[115] He may have had a soft spot

114 The official liberation was 5th May 1945; see www.scrapbookpages.com/Mauthausen/KZMauthausen/Liberation/index.html
115 All opioids are very constipating, so opium would have this effect too, no doubt.

for Chava, for he gave her a comb. After all, her hair was already two centimetres long.

One day an SS woman guard was caught trying to escape in civilian clothes. She was carrying a suitcase. The US soldiers threw the suitcase to Chava and the rest. When it burst open, the contents appeared unbelievable: underwear, shirts and a phonograph and records! It seemed to them as if they were now millionaires. But Chava's thoughts were not there, just with her loved ones and home.

She had no hope for her mother's survival, but there was still that hope that somehow her father might have survived. But it was not to be. Sadly she did not feel able to pray, though she recognised that it might have been a help.

While they were waiting to leave the camp, the American soldiers could not do enough for them and gave them cigarettes all the time. On one occasion they walked to the local village. The walk through the trees and scenery was wonderful. They went to a local monastery and were fed with spinach and semolina dumplings. An American soldier made the baker in the village give Chava and the others bread.

It was during this time that Chava got her first marriage proposal from 'her' Frenchman, who wanted to whisk her off to Paris.

Those early days of liberation were like a trance. To Chava they felt unreal and dreamlike, as if she were but a spectator. But it did not last, for one had to think of the future and she knew for sure that whatever awaited her, she would be going to Eretz.[116] There was no other place for her.

On about 20th May Chava started her journey home on board a boat. The boat only got as far as Tulln, where it had to stop as there was a bombed bridge blocking its passage. Chava and her sister decided to try to make their own way home. They discovered that there was a train to Vienna and, having sold some of their cigarettes, they bought tickets.

Vienna was in ruins. They tried to get to the Eastern railway station but there were no trains running. A local bus driver would have given them a lift, but he was only going about twenty kilometres.

They met an elderly Jewish-Gentile couple and the woman asked if it was true that they had been beaten in the camps. (Extraordinary, if you

---

116 The full expression is Eretz Israel, and referred to Palestine, as the country was then known.

think about it, that they could not bring themselves to believe what they were told about the camps, even though they themselves must have been subjected to significant discrimination in Vienna.)

A young man adopted them and led them into town. At a Russian checkpoint they were taken by the guard to the officer in charge. Both of these Russians were Jews. The officer ordered the provision of food, a kind of porridge called *Kaska*, and Chava says that despite their hunger it was difficult getting it down. They were then sent to the Jewish community centre, and from there to a hospital from whence they at last got shelter. The young man stayed with them to make sure they would be all right; otherwise he was going to take them home and give up his bed for them. They parted from him with many thanks.

In the morning they went directly to the Jewish community centre, but the only help they got was a food voucher. They decided to eat and then start out on foot for home to Bratislava.

It was starting to rain when they were picked up by someone claiming to be the Mayor of Schwechat (a suburb of Vienna and the location of the present airport). He protested that he had not been a Nazi, and he did take them home and put them up for the night in a small room in the yard, allowing them to wash and giving them food.

The next day they tried again. This time they were offered a lift by some Russians. They had been warned that there was a risk of rape, but they decided to accept anyway. The truck stopped in the middle of nowhere and there was a moment of unease. But in fact it was only so that one of the Russians, who spoke Yiddish, could give them his coat as it was cold.

At last they arrived at a place called Petržalka, which was on the outskirts of Bratislava. There were crowds of people there, but as Chava and Agi had their release papers from Mauthausen they were able to walk across a pontoon bridge into the city. Someone on that bridge told them that their three uncles had been shot – the three who had decided to be baptised.

They headed for their last accommodation prior to deportation, but there was no news of the family. They then went to what had been the 'Braun store',[117] and there found their Uncle Dezsoe with his son Jozo. He

---

117 This originally belonged to Chava's maternal grandparents (surname Braun), and then to her three baptised uncles. In Bratislava the family were known as the '*Mehl* Braun', i.e. the 'flour Browns'.

apologised that all he had was cookies which the mice had got into, and could not understand why they roared with laughter.

From there they went on to Chava's Aunt Mariska, who had survived with 'Aryan papers' and already had a flat. Her aunt knew where Chava's friend Aviva was, and contacted her. Aviva must have rushed round, for Chava was still having a bath when she arrived. Aviva gave her a skirt as they had often exchanged clothes in the past at Čadca, but when Chava tried to put it on it just fell to the ground.

Her grandmother who had been in the hospital at Nitra had also survived and came and stayed with them, but died soon after. Chava says that hers was the first funeral she attended. Prior to that she had just seen piles of corpses. Her parents sadly had not survived, but a few of her friends did – some, like herself, in the camps; others by hiding or with Aryan papers.

Things normalised. Chava travelled to Budapest for a meeting of the remnants of the youth movement. The Red Cross provided the Zionist Youth movement with a villa located in Bratislava, formerly owned by a Jewish family. From there they worked with displaced Jewish children, collecting them off the streets or from wherever they were hidden – convents, forests or Gentile families.

Chava's account ends with words which are a most moving testimony to her.

I do not know how to end these notes – is there a moral? Vengeance, retribution, hate? I never believed in these – they cannot bring back what we have lost! The only moral is, to cherish life, every day that I can freely breathe – all the rest is unimportant! I feel that each day I have lived until today is a present.

While Chava was working with the displaced Jewish children in 1946, a young man, Max Lieben (now Livni), became manager of the home for children and young people where she was already working. They fell in love and married.

Max had a very different background to hers. He came from Prague. His family were very Orthodox, though his personal viewpoint came to differ from theirs. He had also had a hard time. He was deported to Theresienstadt, and from there to Auschwitz. After about ten days he and his brother Rudi noticed that there was a group of prisoners who were being made ready for departure to a work camp. Somehow they managed to join this group and left Auschwitz, ending up at a camp in Kaufering. Max was an electrician, a skill which was in demand at least some of the time, but conditions were nevertheless terrible. Sadly Rudi fell ill in December 1944 and died of consumption. Max himself contracted typhoid, but survived it. After the war and liberation he returned to Prague, where he found that of the dozens of family members who had remained in Europe, only three had survived.

Chava and Max were anxious to emigrate to Israel, but circumstances prevented it and it was not until April 1949 that they were at last allowed to do so. They initially lived on a kibbutz but it was not a happy experience, especially for Chava, and in 1951 they moved to Kiryat Tiv'on.

Chava had recorded that when she was in the camps she wondered whether she would ever be able to have children. I am happy to say that she did, though sadly her eldest child Eli contracted polio in 1953 and died that year. Her two daughters, Nurit and Liora, have married and Chava now has grandchildren and great-grandchildren.